MW00936101

GOD'S GOLD!

A JOURNEY OF DISCOVERY

VOLUME 1 AND VOLUME 2

(VOLUME 1)

FINDING GOLD IN MOTHER LODE QUARTZ VEINS, AND "GOD'S GOLD" IN THE BOOK OF DANIEL

&

(VOLUME 2)

"THE JOURNEY CONTINUES"

ISBN:1502451638

ED AND JIM

THIS BOOK IS PRESENTED TO:

Bill

FROM:

MIKE DARBY

209 736-00 44

ON THE DATE OF:

8/26/15

ON THE OCCASION OF:

FRIENDS —

CONTENTS

VOLUME 1
Discovering Gold in Mother Lode Quartz Veins, and *"God's Gold"* in the Book of Daniel

ACKNOWLEDGMENTS

**Jesus, thank you
for letting me discover the
wonders of your mysteries.**

PART 1

THE

DISCOVERY

A Mysterious Pattern In The Flow of Western History
What Does it Mean?

Starting from the days of Alexander the Great, until the year 2000, *Seven Empires* have ruled the Western World in consecutive order. The lineup goes like this:

The *Greek Empire*. . .

The *Roman Empire*. . .

The *Byzantine Empire*. . .

The *Carolingian Empire*. . .

(*Charlemagne's family bloodline*). . .

The Carolingians were followed by the

Venetian Empire (*the Crusader period*). . .

The *Sixth*, was the *Dual Empire* of the

Portuguese and *Spanish*. . .

And lastly, the British Empire. . .

But here's the interesting thing. . .

The successive *'Rise and Fall'* of each Empire, has repeated, like clockwork, every 333.33 years. . .

. . . It really has!

Wow!

HISTORY CHART

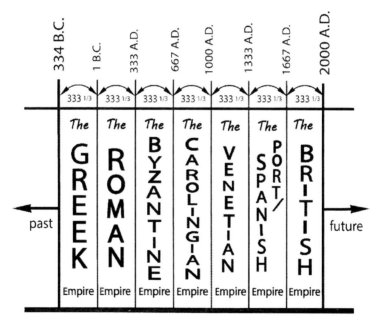

The Seven Empires of Western Civilization

What does this mysterious pattern mean?. .

Can it predict the future?. .

Will yet *another* empire rise, and be destined to rule for 333.33 more years?. .

What the *h#*k* is going on here?

Believe it or not, this pattern, has *everything to do* with the *Second Coming Of Jesus Christ!* I'll explain as we go. . .

[If you like, you can take a *'sneak peek'* at the *expanded explanation* of this pattern. Just go forward to page 129, read a few pages, then come back here.]

Hi, I'm Mike Darby. . . And I discovered this intriguing pattern back in 1992, while attending a biblical studies course, on the Big Island of Hawaii. My discovery began from a *study* that I was making in the book of Daniel. When I discovered the pattern, it was like finding a pocket of gold in a Mother Lode quartz vein. As I dug deeper into the vein, I kept finding more pockets of gold!

Digging For Gold
For Real!

Now when I say; *"it was like discovering a pocket of gold"* I know what I'm talking about. . . Here's a picture of me looking out of my tunnel, where I found gold!

You can buy gold, but you can't *buy* the discovery. . .

I'm a 'Discoverer'. . . It's what I do. . . You can buy gold, but you can't buy the discovery. It takes *more than money*. . . Yet, at the same time, it may take *no money at all*. . . But it *always* takes *faith*. . .

Notice, that I didn't say; *"I'm an Explorer"*. . . But I actually said; *"I'm a Discoverer. . ."*

There were lots of *'Explorer's'* travelling around in the 1500's, but Columbus was a *Discoverer!* An 'Explorer' *Seeks*, but a 'Discoverer' *Finds*. So whether you're looking for *Gold*, or looking for *God's Wisdom*, the principals are exactly the same. . .

Now of course, you can't be a very successful *'Discoverer,'* without *first* being an *'Explorer.'* And you can't really be a *'finder,'* without first being a *'Seeker.'* The only difference between an *'Explorer'* and a *'Discoverer,'* is that the *'Discoverer'* keeps on seeking until he finds. And *that* my friend is the difference!

A few years ago, at an old mine site near my home in the Mother Lode town of Angels Camp California, I was searching around the hillside for quartz veins to sample. I found a narrow vein of quartz rock near the surface of the ground, so I dug out a sample. The vein was only around 1/2" to 1" wide, but after testing the sample of rock, I discovered that it was carrying traces of *"free"* gold.

Over the next few weeks and months, I picked, and I dug, and I hammered and chiseled my way through nearly twenty five feet of dirt and rock. Leaving behind this 12-14 ft. tunnel in the side of the mountain. I kept finding gold in that vein the whole way!

But after the twenty five foot quest, the vein looked like it was *'playing out,'* so I decided to put the chase on the back burner. I slowed it down a bit, but continued to take samples from the tunnel every now and then. Meanwhile, winter hit. . . There was a *'cave in'* at the entrance of the tunnel, and a pool of water and mud filled the inside floor (not to mention a hundred-and-one *other* distractions that came along during that time.) But something makes me want to get back out there, and keep chasing it again. I want to find a pocket in that vein.

I can expect to find a pocket of gold somewhere in the neighborhood of 5-10 ounces or possibly even more! A 1910 county mining report recorded a ten pound pocket of gold, in the same hillside where I've been digging.

The type of mining I'm doing here is called: *'Pocket Mining'*. The important thing to remember in *'Pocket Mining'* is this; If there is still a quartz vein showing (in other words, if it hasn't *'pinched out' or disappeared*), and if there are still traces of *free gold* in the vein, then there is *still* the potential of finding a pocket. . . So keep digging!

Pocket mining works like this; The quartz veins run in streaks through the bedrock like frosting between layers of cake. First you dig out some of the quartz material from a vein. Then, you put the rock sample in a bag to take home and test for gold. I usually use a sandbag or canvas sack. If I'm taking multiple samples from different veins, I label the bags with numbers and put a note in each bag telling where it came from and giving a short description of the vein (the *last* thing that you want to do is to find gold in one of your sample bags, but not know where it came from).

Next, we take the rock samples back home, and soak them in buckets of water over night or for a few days (sometimes there's a lot of clay in the rock samples which will need to be dissolved before you can *'pan out'* the samples).

Now comes the moment of truth. . . Using a big galvanized washtub, we pan through the samples with a gold pan. Hopefully we find something. . . Even a trace amount. We then compare the samples, and keep digging where we find the most *"color"* (particles and pieces of gold). Generally, if there is any gold in the vein, we will begin to find a consistent trail of particles running through a section of the vein. This trail is called; *'The Lead.'* You have to *'follow the lead,'* because the *'Lead,'* leads to the pocket! At least that's the hope. . .

If you like, you can go to my website: www.goldrushoriginals.com and watch my demonstration on *Hard Rock Gold Mining.*

God's Gold
It's All About Discovery!

God's Gold is *all about* Discovery . . . Sure, this book is about discovering quartz gold in the *California Mother Lode Gold Country*. . .   But it's *mainly* about a set of discoveries I made from the book of Daniel, while I was living in Hawaii. You see, I was contemplating a mysterious numerological vision (recorded in the 8th Chapter of Daniel), when I found a fascinating *'Three-Way-Connection'* between *"Alexander the Great - 2300 years - and the 1967 Six-Day-War* in the Middle East" (which I explain in detail on pages 60-62.) That *initial discovery* from Daniel Chapter 8, paved the way for a *whole set* of *other* amazing discoveries (one of which, was the intriguing *'Pattern of The Seven Empires of Western Civilization.'*)

As you read *"God's Gold!"* you'll also notice an *inspiring theme* running through it. The *theme is* about: *'Discovery itself,'* or better yet, *'The "Path" of Discovery'*. . . In other words, whether we're looking for *gold* in a Mother Lode hillside, or trying to discover *God's hidden wisdom*, the principles are exactly the same. . . Keep *searching*, and don't quit *"following the lead"*. .

Dave's Biggest Pocket Of Gold
In The Swastika Vein!

My mining partner, longtime friend, and *gold mining mentor* is Dave from New York. He moved to California from Brooklyn in the late seventies and settled in Angels Camp. Dave taught me the *dying art* of pocket mining. He also told me about the secret location of the hillside mine, which he in turn learned from a couple of guys that he met shortly after moving to Angels Camp. Their names were *Chris*, and *Guy*.

Chris was Serbian, and *Guy* was Cornish/Welsh. The two men had been lifelong friends, growing up in Angels Camp. As young men in their 20's (possibly even teens) Chris and Guy worked in management level capacities at some of the mines around Angels Camp. When Guy was young (in his 20's?), he was in charge of the *120 stamp mill* at the Carson Hill Gold Mine just outside of Angels Camp. Carson Hill is where they discovered one of the Largest gold nuggets in the world! Chris was the foreman at another mine between Carson hill and Angels Camp.

They worked in mines in the 1920's and 30's, but something unusual happened in 1941. When America entered World War II, the U.S. Congress passed a resolution which essentially shut down all of the hard-rock gold mines, Most of the big (investor backed) mines in California never recovered after the War. There were a few reasons for this.

Many of the Mother Lode mines became flooded with water as soon as they shut down in 1941. The *"start-up"* costs alone, for just pumping out the water, were staggering. Many of the Patented Mining claims (properties owned by the mining companies) were sold off to private individuals like cattle ranchers. But even after the war years were over, Chris and Guy continued to mine, and look for gold on their own. Growing up, they had acquired a lot of knowledge about lots of places. They knew where *all the good places were*, because they had worked at many of those places when they were younger, or else they had heard reliable stories about certain places from others who had worked them. At any rate, searching for gold became a lifelong quest for Chris and Guy.

Dave worked with Chris and Guy for nearly *twenty years*, and learned all he could from them. Dave likes to give names to the quartz veins that he is taking samples from. He started doing this so it would be easier for him to remember and keep track of where his samples came from. There is nothing worse than collecting a bunch of rock samples from a number of different veins, only to have one test positive for gold, but not know where the sample came from! It's happened to Dave, and it has happened to me as well.

One particular time, Dave and Chris were out at the *hillside mine*, and Dave found *visible gold* right at the surface in a ¾" wide vein! They chased the vein down over the next ten days or so, digging a trench about thirteen feet deep. They found seven ounces all together. But then, at the bottom of the trench, the vein made two sharp turns. . .

Now when Dave first told me the story of this discovery, he got to that point of the story, then looked at me (kind-a funny like) and said; "the vein made *two sharp turns* at the bottom, just like a *"Swastika!"* (Dave is a Jewish guy from Brooklyn, and with quite a sense of humor, I might add.) Anyway, right there, between the two turns, was a eighteen ounce pocket of gold! It was the biggest pocket of gold he has ever found to date.

Oh the irony. . . Dave, the *Jewish guy* from Brooklyn, finds the biggest pocket of gold in his life, right in the middle of a *"Swastika"* vein! So they found a total of twenty five ounces of gold on the *"Swastika Vein."* The biggest piece of gold was about the size of a golf ball. Not only that, but there's another thing to consider. . . The gold from that particular place is fabulous specimen gold, and can be worth *way more* than its own weight, depending on the specimen. It's a beautiful, bright, light yellow, crystalline gold. One of the specimens (from the eighteen ounce pocket) looked just like butterfly wings. . .

Now they were a three-way partnership, so Guy had a share coming as well. He ended up taking the *golf-ball-size* piece. What a discovery! And today, I have the privilege of mining in the very same spot. So, in a sense, Dave has passed the *'mantle'* on to me.

The Daniel Vein
And The Return Of Christ

My *"Journey of Discovery"* on the *Daniel Vein* was just like *'following the lead'* on a vein of quartz, that was carrying multiple pockets of gold.

The *'Daniel Vein'* has kept me occupied for years now. . . And it has become for me a rich and productive gold mine, full of profound biblical insight and revelation, about the *flow of History* and the *Second Coming of Christ*. . . And I'm ready now to share with you, some of those Insights and Revelations.

In the pages to follow, I'll tell you all about these things, and at the same time, share a few stories about Hard Rock mining, as well as *more* of my thoughts about *"The Path of Discovery."*

The Fast Track By-Pass
A Quicker Way

By-the-way. . . Just as I was getting ready to publish *GOD'S GOLD!*, I learned of an interesting statistic. Apparently, 90% of *all* readers, finish only 10% of any book that they begin to read (now those numbers may *actually* be closer to 80% and 20%, *but still*. . .)

Not only do I want you to *finish* reading *"GOD'S GOLD!,"* but I'd like you to tell a friend about it as well. . . Aside from selling my book, I *really* want people share in the excitement, and understand the unique discoveries I've made on the *'Daniel Vein.'* So I've come up with a couple ways to help make that happen. First, there's the *"Fast Track By-Pass to Discovery."*

The *"Fast-Track By-Pass. . ."* shortens *"GOD'S GOLD"* by about 38%. It lets you by-pass the *gold mining stories*, and *memoirs* about my *journey on the 'Path of Discovery,'* so that you can focus *exclusively* on the discoveries that I made on the *'Daniel Vein.'*

So If you feel like the book is a bit *sluggish*, or you want to *By-Pass* all the other stuff, then simply jump onto the:

"FAST-TRACK, BY-PASS TO DISCOVERY > > >"
(Starting On Page 48.

And if that's not enough, you can go one step further. . . Near the end of this book, on page 335, I've created a condensed overview, listing seven of my *key* discoveries from the *"Daniel Vein."* The list outlines a quick explanation of each discovery, so you can get the 'big picture' *Super-Fast*.

If *"GOD'S GOLD!"* were a textbook, the *'Condensed Overview List'* would be like the *'answers section'* at the back of a teachers edition. So don't spoil the fun of reading *"GOD'S GOLD!"* by reading the *"Condensed List"* first. rather, use the list as you need it, or as an overview, after you've read *"GOD'S GOLD!"* in its entirety.

On the other hand. . . .   The *'Condensed Overview List'* is there for you, *anytime* you need it. . .

Discovery Is Beyond Our Control
The Walk Of Faith

Discovery is beyond the control of its Discoverer. . . But the Discoverer *definitely* has a hand in it, nonetheless. But when *God* is in the mix, it's a guaranteed success! The book of Proverbs (Chapter 25:2) tells us that God does the job of *hiding* things, and he gives *us* the Job of discovering them! The New Testament explains this principal over and over, using many different illustrations. In fact, the Old Testament of the Bible does so as well. It's the way of *Faith --- "FAITH IN GOD"*.

I'm not talking about faith in *'yourself,'* or faith in *'other people,'* or faith in *'another god'*, or even faith (as some like to put it) *"in the Universe"*! I'm talking about *Faith* in the *God of the Bible* (the traditional God of the people of Israel, the God of Christians). If *that* God is in the mix, then you can expect success. But you need to walk in *FAITH*.

King Solomon, In all of his wisdom said: *"Quit dreaming and DO SOMETHING!"*

Ecclesiastes 5:3 say's; "A dream comes to its fulfillment through a lot of hard work, but you can easily tell who the fool is. . . *He's* the one who only *talks* about his dreams!" [my paraphrase].

If you're dreaming about a lifestyle of *Discovery,* then start *Living The Dream!* Know that anything is possible with God, but *do something about it.* Start living *"The Supernatural Lifestyle Provided By Jesus Christ."*

In the book of Hebrews (Chapter Eleven) it says that God rewards people who seek him with diligence. God is pleased with that kind of person. There are *some* out there who would have you believe that the only thing God requires. . . is nothing at all.[63] Good Luck! . . But I've found that if the *seed* of faith has sprouted in your heart, then you must give to it, all that it is requiring of you i.e. courage, intelligence, strength etc., or you run the risk of *'losing out'* on your reward from God. . .

Now sometimes, all we need to do is *"ask".* The book of James tells us that we don't *"have"* because we're not *"asking. . ."*[64] Jesus taught (in the sermon on the mount) that if we'll *ask,* then we'll *receive.* And if we *seek,* we'll *find.* And if we persistently *"knock",* then the door will be opened up for us.

So who's giving?.. Who's letting us find? And who's opening the door for us? . . . God!

Notice the acronym?

A = ASK

S = SEEK

K = KNOCK

That's pretty neat isn't it!   I read those passages starting in Matthew 7:7 for years, but never noticed the acronym till this wonderful black lady pointed it out to me. . . (I don't know her name, or I would give her credit for her discovery). Notice that the three actions (ask, seek, knock) are all passive (in the sense that they are motivated from our "need"), but they are *also* aggressive, because they require action on our part. . . And not just *any old kind of action*, but *"persistent"* action! Do you want something from God?   He rewards those who *"diligently"* seek him.

Whatever it is that we're searching for from God, our natural propensity is to *"give up,"* or to *"loose hope."* The tendency is start thinking that doesn't care about what *we* want, or that we're being too much of a *"pest"* to God. You can't let *that kind* of mentality keep you from knocking on his door till he answers it for you. . . (Luke 11:5-10).

Wilma's Miracle
"The Overhaul"

One evening, around thirty years ago, I was at a meeting of the *"Full Gospel Businessmen's Fellowship International"* in the town of San Andreas (which is about eleven miles northwest of Angels Camp on highway 49). There was a lady (Wilma) from Angels Camp at the meeting who looked as though she was on-her-way-out of this world. She was naturally a *big boned* woman, but that night she weighed only 65 lbs. or less. Wilma looked like a survivor from a Nazi concentration camp! She had been a heavy drinker, and now she was wasting away because her liver was dead (Cirrhosis of the liver). I didn't really know Wilma at that time, but I recognized that she was someone from Angels Camp.

"Bill" was the guest speaker that night. He was an evangelist from the Mother Lode area (Placerville). And he was telling stories that night about Miracle services which he had conducted recently in the Philippines. At the end of the meeting, a friend took Wilma up front to get prayer from Bill. I happened to be standing there when Wilma (in a light hearted way) explained to Bill that she simply needed an overhaul. Bill said: Lord, please give this woman an overhaul!

I didn't think any more about it. But about a year later, I bumped into Wilma at the hardware store. I didn't recognize who she was until she explained to me that she was the lady at the Full Gospel Businessmen's meeting in San Andreas, that was prayed for by Bill from Placerville. Her liver starting working again, and she had gained back at least a hundred pounds! She was back to normal again, and even better than before! Unbelievable! Wilma *ASKED*, and she *RECIEVED!*

You Reap What You Sow
An Eye-Opening Experience

When I saw Wilma in the hardware store that day, she told me that she couldn't find anyone who wanted to work (like help clean up around her yard.) So I volunteered.

During those days, I was on a special quest. I had begun an intense campaign of fasting, praying, and sacrificial giving (helping out poor people, widows and orphans etc. (James 1:27). I had been listening to a lot of Christian teachings about the fact that, "if you *give*, then you will *receive*, and if you *sow*, then you will *reap. . ."*

Now the *principle* was supposed to work, whether you sow good things or evil things. And if you *sow bountifully*, then you will also *reap bountifully!* Nowadays, people *allude* to this principle when they say; *"What goes around comes around."*

There was *also* a lot of talk going around, back in those days, about a *"hundred fold reward"* (which comes out of Jesus' parable of the *wheat harvest*. And passages like Mark 10:31, and Matthew 19:29, where Jesus spoke of receiving 'a *hundred times*' in houses and lands. . . ." if they have been forfeited on *his* behalf" etc.) So (based on this thinking), the idea was going around the Christian community, that if you *"sow"* a *dollar*, then you could potentially *"reap back"* a *hundred bucks*. So for some folks, it started to become sort of a Christian *"get rich quick scheme."*

But Hey!. . . It *all* sounded pretty good to me! I wasn't necessarily *sold out* on all the ideas behind the *"100X Reward"* teaching, but I was *curious* to see what kind of *harvest* would come back to me, if I threw myself into an intense season of trying to do nothing but *good works* by *Faith!* So I embarked on a quest to that end. . . .

Well, I didn't know any *Orphans*, but Wilma seemed to qualify in the category of *"Widows,"* So besides a bunch of other *good things* I was doing at that time, I began helping Wilma do stuff around her house.

Now I can tell you *this*;. . . about six months later, I saw a harvest. I *definitely* saw a reward for *all* the specific things that I had been doing. I couldn't tell if there was a 30X, 60X, or 100X reward, but I *absolutely* saw distinct rewards which were all based directly upon my actions! There was a new automobile, a new dwelling, a new Job, and new friends, etc.

I don't have the space right now, to explain *exactly* what I'm talking about, but It was *weird!* And at first, it kind of *'freaked me out'* a little bit! Because after that experience, in a *new* kind of way, it became very clear to me, that *my actions* actually *have a hand* in determining *things* that will eventually *come my way* in life. In other words, I should be careful what I "sow" (as well as how bountifully I "sow"), because. . . . *"What I sow, I will reap!"*

One Of My Strangest Discoveries

"The Mud-Dauber Miracle"

One day (at Wilma's), I was knocking down hundreds of "Mud-Dauber" nests from off of the rafters in her garage. Mud-Daubers are a type of wasp that make nests out of mud. While I was taking a break I picked up one of the mud dauber's nests from the garage floor and began to contemplate its design. I noticed that the Mud Dauber nest looked like a little *"eight pack"* cluster of hand-made pots (like ancient pottery from the Mediterranean or Middle East). Immediately my *creative gift* began to operate. I started to imagine. . . What if I made little pots, that looked like ancient urns (but made out of real gold). They could become beautiful ladies necklaces. . .

See how it looks like a little ancient clay pot! The actual size of the Mud Dauber pottery is: about 1" in length.

Then, I began to think: "If only I had access to a dental lab, then I could cast one up in gold, and see what it would look like!"

I happened to know that dentists cast gold tooth crowns the same way jewelers cast pieces of jewelry. I had a pretty good friend at the time who was a dentist, but I didn't think he would go for the idea of helping me cast a Mud Dauber pot into gold in his dental lab. . . . Then, about five minutes later, I noticed a door connected to a *side room* of the garage, and I was wondered what was on the other side. So I proceeded to open the door, and to my surprise, *'lo and behold'*, inside that room was a dental lab!!! What-wer-th-chances?

I immediately asked Wilma about it, but my wonderful rapture, *ruptured,* when she told me to *"forget about it"*! The owner, she said, was coming out from Arizona to pick it up, like, immediately, or something. . .

That was weird! What a bummer! How perplexing! What a tease! Now I *really* wanted to see this *gold pottery thing* happen, so I prayed *'in the Spirit,'*[62] then I prayed out loud: "Lord, I want to see what one of these little pots look like cast in gold! Can you please get me access to a *dental lab* or something?!! I figured I'd just have to wait for *"some other day"*, or *"some other dental lab?"*

Now here's the weird part. . . Two days later, I was visiting a friend, *'Marguerite,'* she was another one of those people on my list, who qualified in the category of *'Widows.' She* didn't need yard work, or anything like that, but she was mostly just lonely, and liked talking with me about biblical and spiritual things (sometimes, for hours on end). I didn't mind talking to her, but the *sacrifice* was that it seemed like I was wasting away my own precious productivity time. *Marguerite* was an elderly lady who had been an artist for many years, and was now going blind.

During our conversation, that particular day, I asked Marguerite if she had any wood carving tools, and if so, could I use them? (I had been wanting to *try my hand* at carving some *"soapstone".*)

So after hearing my request, she said absolutely, then she told me that there was a little wooden box containing a set of carving tools, out in her garage, on top of her water heater. Sure enough, I found the box on top of the water heater, but when I went to open up the box, I noticed that it was glued shut by Mud-Daubers. But when I finally broke it open to look at the tools, I found an amazing surprise inside.

In between a few of the carving tools sticking up here and there, was a *Mud-Dauber* nest. And one of the *little pots* on that nest was *METALIC SILVER!!!* It wasn't gold, but it was *metal. . .*

I thought that it was some kind of *"Creative Miracle."* It looked like the Lord had turned one of those little clay *Mud-Dauber* pot into *silver* just for me. . . But why wasn't it gold? . . . It didn't really matter. . . It was metal nonetheless.

After a few minutes I discovered a can of metallic aluminum roofing paint, which had fallen off a shelf in the room, and it was oozing out into a puddle on the floor. Half of the silver paint was drying out at about the same consistency as the mud that is harvested by Mud-Dauber wasps when they are building their nests! The silver paint was *perfect* material for the Mud-Daubers, who apparently didn't care if the color was *silver* or *brown*, nor if it smelled like *paint* rather than *mud*!

My conclusion, was that the *silver pot* was *not* the product of a *Creative Miracle*. But I believe that God answered my prayer nonetheless. In *this case*, it didn't have to be *Supernatural* to be *Miraculous*. It was pretty close though. I mean, what are the chances? I took it as a *sign* from the Lord, that he wanted me to pursue a path of *Artistic Creativity!* Which I did. . .

Another time (recently), I was asking the Lord to heal me from *Springtime Allergies*. Conventional medicine made me feel *worse* than the allergies themselves. I didn't think there I was a cure, but shortly thereafter, I found a cure! I discovered three separate ways to do it through *Natural Medicine*. . . And it worked!!! Absolutely!!! It wasn't supernatural (like Wilma's miracle), but it was *definitely* an answer to my prayer.

Whatever we're searching for, our natural tendency is to *"give up"*, *"loose hope"*, but *keep seeking, and you will find*. . . Whatever it is that you're looking for, keep on asking, and it will be given to you! Whether it's *discovering gold* in Mother Lode Quartz veins, or discovering the cure for your *Spring Time allergies*, or even discovering a *Pattern in the Flow of History* that produces evidence that the *Return of Christ* is really going to happen, the principle is exactly the same. *Ask, Seek, and Knock!*

PART 2

THE

PATH OF

DISCOVERY

Who Am I?
I'm A Discoverer!

I've worn many labels in my life. I've even worn some of those labels out, LOL! I've been known as; an "Artist", a "Jack of all trades", and even a "Renaissance Man". I've been tagged with some negatives as well... i.e. *'Starving Artist'*, *'Lazy'*, *'Crazy'*, and *'Dreamer. . .'* I use to have a hard time finding the right classification to define myself . . . (who I am, and what I do.) For a while there, I was calling myself; a *'Multi-Faceted Individual'*. . . But that sounded too much like *'Multiple Personality.'* So if *you* were *me*, how would you define yourself?

Please bear with me while I talk about "ME" for a few moments. . . When I was a kid (fifth grade) I discovered how to make gunpowder from three basic ingredients. Fortunately, I never set the town on fire. I discovered things like; how to make hydrogen (which *itself* is highly flammable, and explosive). Helium filled Balloons were a rare commodity back then. They were only to be found once a year at the county fair. But my hydrogen discovery allowed my friends and I access to year round flotation fun! My favorite book was an Encyclopedia.

I researched Tesla Coils[1], made Leyden Jars[2], and played around with magnets and electric motors.

And I was always 'really good' at drawing. . . everybody called me Michelangelo, but my real hero as a kid was Leonardo da Vinci. . . As I grew older, I became a proficient musician (instrumentalist, singer, songwriter). I may have spent way too much time trying to crack the code for 'anti-gravity'! (be easy on me now, I'm baring my heart here!). . . I had a million different jobs by the time I was twenty six years old, but in 1989 (after working 1 year with a carpet cleaning & dying company), I officially went into self-employment cleaning and repairing oriental rugs in New Orleans.

Later that same year, I found myself designing needlepoint rugs with a startup company in Uptown New Orleans. It was then that I believed I had found my life's vocation. . . I was now a "Rug Designer"! One of my rug designs actually made it into the industry's most prestigious awards competition (the 'Roscoe Awards'), and we began selling rugs with that particular design through a 'high end' San Francisco Mail Order Catalog Company. . . What a rush!

Now, I wasn't born or raised "Up Town". . . And I was never an Up-Town Kind-of-a-Guy, but it sure was a kick for me back then, Hob-Nob'n with people like "Mr. Spaghetti Sauce" (who had turned his *own* father's spaghetti sauce business into a nationally recognized name brand). "Mr. Spaghetti Sauce" was the father of one of the owners of the rug company. One of Mr. Spaghetti Sauce's favorite sayings went like this; *Sell to the Classes, and live with the masses. Sell to the masses and live with the Classes.* Everybody buys spaghetti sauce. . . He was a real *'shaker and a mover,'* and he became fabulously wealthy. His home looked like the Vatican. All of the doors in his house were hand carved and covered in gold leaf. . . And he had a life size statue of Jesus (from an old Catholic Church) in one of the main rooms of his residence (I think it was in the living room!)

You know... there have been *scores* of Priests and Monks throughout history who have literally taken vows of poverty. . . But I can tell you right now, that I never actually had to try very hard to be poor. . .

I've been broke most of my life! LOL!!!

There was lot of wealth back there, but I couldn't get much of it to stick to me. . .

But if nothing else, I gained a lot of valuable experience and knowledge. And in all actuality, I believe I had to leave that world behind in order to move on to a greater level of *discovery*. . .

My involvement in the rug business eventually led me into the world interior-design art. I began doing faux painting on walls, then *'Trompe L'oi'* [3] and murals. I started playing around with plaster, and discovered a unique way to create large plaster relief sculpture murals that have the appearance of bronze, silver, or gold (see page 44.)

But how did I *start out* cleaning carpets, and *end up* becoming a sculptor, and eventually a Gold Miner, Adventure Tour Guide, and now (I suppose) an Author? . . . It was the path of *discovery*!

It's *All* About Discovery
Start Living The Dream!

You may have heard the old adage; *Find something you're good at, and do it!* In other words, find a level of proficiency, then grow and multiply on that level, and success will follow. I've found that you can grow *outward* or *upward*s. . .

A number of years ago, I met a guy who lives in my home town and who had been in the carpet cleaning business for fifteen or twenty years. He and I started around the same time, and he was making a *really good* living (better than I was at the time). I was sort of envious, thinking: "I could have done that!" But I had taken another path. . . Instead of growing *"out-ward"* on that level, I chose to grow *"up-ward."* For decades now, I've kept being drawn upwards, to higher and higher levels of creative endeavor and *discovery.*

It's the *Path. . . . . . of Discovery!*

Every time I *mastered* a certain level of proficiency in one area, I would always seem to find myself wanting to *'punch through'* to a new level. . . The pay scale is always better on the higher level, and the perks and bonuses are more rewarding, but it comes with a price. . .

The *Downside* to this kind of lifestyle is that you *may* have to make financial concessions. . . And those *concessions* oftentimes appear to others, to be a reflection on your own *"lack of intelligence."* You may oftentimes be misunderstood, because unfortunately, sometimes, in order to break into a new level, you just have to *'let go'* of that precious financial security that comes from being able to *branch out* and *multiply* on a single level of proficiency. Remember this; The money must always come later, but the *choice to move up* always comes first. . . So how high do you want to fly? The choice is up to you!

According to King Solomon, The *signature crown* of the wise are their riches. . . A crown is the symbol of Authority. It means that you *know* what you're talking about. Therefore, according to King Solomon, wealth is an *indicator* of true intelligence. In another Proverb, Solomon *also* explained that the wise inherit immediate honor.

If you *do the math* and *read between the lines,* you should be able to figure it out; When attempting to go down a path of discovery, you may end up butting heads with concerned family members or friends. . . But wisdom is vindicated by her children. . . So how high do you want to go?

I love Geometry, History, Jesus, and the Bible. I want to go to the Holy Land and re-trace the footsteps of Moses, Peter and the Apostle Paul. I invented and produced a family card game called: "Inspector Pancake"™ The details of the game came to me in a dream one night around Valentine's Day. I've had a number of prophetic dreams over the years. . .

One particular dream I had, led me to open up a small shop in my home town in Angels Camp, where I take people out on gold panning adventure tours. It's also my art studio. At the shop, I paint murals on gold pans, and in my '*miners laboratory*', I mess around *"Electra-Growing"* copper on rocks full of quartz crystals! I grow the copper on the rocks. Then, I *Electro-Plate* the copper with gold, in order to produce fabulous looking museum quality *'faux'* gold specimens. It sounds fun, doesn't it!

Some of my creations at my studio in Angels Camp

Some of my Interior design
relief sculpture work...

Inspector Pancake

Here (above) is the my card game. *"Inspector Pancake™" takes you back in time, to a by-gone era of organized crime. . ."* Four Italian gangster families; *Fettucine, Rigatoni, Spaghetti, and Macaroni. . .* Deal out seven cards, play a series of hands, keeping score as you go. And as soon as any player reaches 100 points, the game is over and the *guy* with the *lowest* number of points wins!

Discoverers are oftentimes mistaken for a Dreamers. . . Now of course, *all* Discoverer's are Dreamer's, but a Discover is *more* than just a "Dreamer. " A Discoverer *"lives the Dream. . ."*

I'm not perfect, by any means. At least not yet. But now, after hearing my trumpet solo, how would you define who I am? Maybe you're just like me. Or, maybe you would like to be *more* like me. . .

Forget trying to figure out all of the complicated
details of life. . .
Just concentrate on being a *Discoverer!*

All right, enough about *me.* Let's get into the good stuff. . .

PART 3

THE

FLOW OF

HISTORY

FAST-TRACK, BY-PASS TO DISCOVERY > > >
Begin here,
and continue reading to page 89:

Millennial Pizza™

A Proportional view of History

A story is told about the legendary baseball player; Joe DiMaggio. Apparently, Joe used to frequent a certain pizza parlor in New York City when he was playing games in the local stadium there. Hey Joe! The owner would ask; "How do you want me to cut your pizza tonight, six pieces or eight?" Then Joe would answer, saying something like; "I'm pretty hungry tonight, you'd better cut it into twelve pieces!" Joe and his friend in the pizza business had quite a sense of humor didn't they!

But the truth is, no matter how you slice a pizza you can't change the sum of its parts. Now I'm not sure if the story is fact or fiction, but we'll use the story here to help explain something called: 'Millennialism'[4].

"Millennialism" is a *'belief system'*, held by Christian believers going all the way back to the first century A.D.

The Ancient Millennial Christian's believed that the flow of history is following a 7000 year cycle (seven millennial days)[5] and that Jesus will return at the end of the 'SIXTH MILLENNIUM' and rule the world for a thousand years from the city of JERUSALEM. It's like a great big seven day week, and each day of this week lasts one thousand years. . .

After the last thousand years are over, a new heavens and a new earth will be made. The ultimate hope of every believer is to be raised to life when Jesus returns... To live and reign with him in his thousand year kingdom... And then, to 'live on' with him in the *New World* which is to come... Again, this ancient Christian Worldview is called:

"Millennialism"[4].

Now, if you could imagine 'Millennial history' in terms of a pizza, what do you think it would look like. . . a 'seven thousand' year old pizza? Not exactly, but it might look something like this:

Each slice represents 1,000 years (a total of 7000 years altogether). Notice the chopped garlic on the very top layer of the pizza? Before I baked it, I added the garlic and drizzled it with Extra Virgin *'first cold pressed'* olive oil. Those two ingredients make all the difference. . . I have to say, it was an excellent pizza. I had the pleasure of eating it, just after the photo shoot for these illustrations! All right, I'll get back to the story. . .

The seven pieces of pizza here represent the *Seven Millenniums* of world history

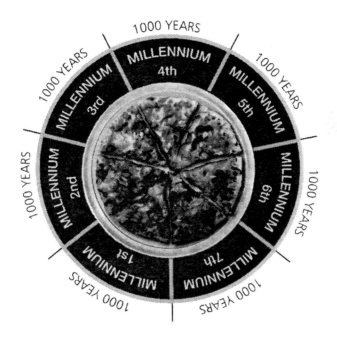

. . . Now for those of you who want to think of the Millennial pizza in a more linear fashion. . .

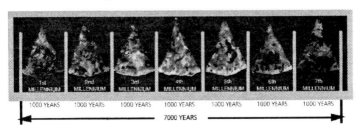

. . .well, you get the idea. . .

But as I mentioned earlier, it makes no difference if we cut the Millennial Pizza into two parts or three, it still adds up to 7000 years.

The word 'Millennialism' comes from the Latin word; mille, and means 'one thousand'. 'Millennialism' is based on the idea that a thousand years are like one day. According to the Prophet Moses, the Heavens and Earth were made in *'six days,'* then on the seventh day, God rested[6]. Therefore the idea follows; that after *'six thousand years'* of world history, a great *'Millennial'* day of rest will also follow (the *'Seventh Millennium'*). During this thousand year period of time, Jesus will rule the world in peace and righteousness, reigning from the City of Jerusalem.

The writings of the Biblical Prophets like Isaiah, Ezekiel, etc. speak marvelous and wonderful things concerning this unique time in the future called *"the Millennium"*. For instance, Isaiah says that "in those days, . . a person who is one hundred years of age will be considered very young.'[7] Another prophecy tells us that 'in those days. . . the City of Jerusalem will have no night time, it will be as daytime there continually.'[8] The City of Jerusalem will become, as it were, the 'Royal City' of Jesus' kingdom on Earth.

Now the Millennial teaching doesn't stop there. . . You see, when the thousand year reign of Christ is over (at the end of the seventh Millennium), a general resurrection from the dead will take place[9]. And all who have ever lived will be raised to life again, and participate in the *'final judgment'* of all things. Then, after these things, a *'new heavens'* and a *'new earth'* will be made, along with a city called the *'New Jerusalem'*[10]. Those who are *'blessed of the Lord'* will inherit these things. The Book of Revelation says that the *'New Jerusalem'* will have streets that are made of *'gold'* like clear glass[11]. Also, the City will have twelve gates, and each one will be made from a single pearl[12]. Hence came the idea that 'Heaven' has *"streets of gold"* and *"pearly gates,"* but Millennialism teaches that the New Jerusalem is a tangible place, which is coming in the future.

And again, not only does Millennialism give us the great and glorious hope of Christ's long awaited return and thousand year reign on this earth, but after the thousand years are over and that last piece of Millennial Pizza has been consumed, a whole new pizza will be coming out of the oven! In other words, after the *old heavens* and the *old earth* pass away, a *new heavens* and a *new earth* will be made. Now that's something to look forward to! Maybe the *new heavens* and *new earth* will come without anchovies!

According to the Biblical timeline of history, the world is presently around six thousand years old[13]. . . Therefore, according to the Millennial view, we are now living during one of the most important junctures in world history: "We are at the end of Millennial 'DAY SIX' right now. . .

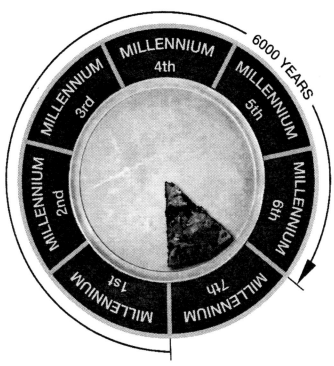

As you can see, there's only one more slice of pizza on the table, but according to the Bible, it's the best slice of all (the *"Seventh Millennium"*). The world has been anticipating that slice of history for the past six thousand years. Evidently, it's just around the corner. . .

Now, at this point, you may be asking the question:

"O.K., but how does all of this *Millennial Pizza* stuff *'tie in'* with the mysterious *Pattern of the Seven Empires,* or the discovery of the *Three-Way-Connection* from the book of Daniel?

That's a good question! Maybe I should start from the beginning, and explain the circumstances that first led me to these discoveries. Come with me now, to the *Big Island of Hawaii*, as I retrace the steps of my discovery. . .

PART 4

THE

QUEST

Aloha

The Trip

I n 1992 I set off with my wife and son, for the Big Island of Hawaii in hopes of discovering some kind of evidence that would support my belief in the *Millennial View* of world history. I planned to take a couple courses at the University of the Nations campus at Kailua-Kona Hawaii.

The U of N is a ministry branch of "Youth With A Mission" or, "YWAM" (which is generally pronounced "why-wam"). YWAM is an inter-denominational short term Christian missionary organization founded by Loren Cunningham and his wife Darlene in 1960. The organization has over 1000 *"bases"* of operation in over 180 countries across the globe.

When we were there in the 90's, the Kailua-Kona Campus was the 'Jewel' of YWAM's family of "bases" (perhaps it still is), and it was the main campus for the *'University of the Nations'* as well as the location of the; *"Office of the Founders."*

The Millennial Hope
My Personal Quest

The first course that I planned to take at YWAM-Kona, was a Biblical studies course. The second was a course in Church history. Each class would take a full year to complete. I planned on staying there two years.

At that time, I didn't even know that the term; *"Millennialism"* even existed. Yet, I had a basic understanding of a 7,000 year cycle, and that Jesus was expected to return around the end of the Sixth Millennium. I also understood that, according to the Biblical timeline, the world is presently at, or near, the *end* of the Sixth Millennium. I'd also heard that there was a pattern in the flow of history, where the major biblical characters like; Adam, Enoch, Noah, Abraham, etc., were equally separated by *500*, or *1000* year spaces of time. . .

My hope was that (after taking both courses at YWAM) I could then build *my own* 6000 year time line of world history, and see if I could find a pattern in the flow of history myself, which would back-up my personal belief in the 'Millennial View'.

Well, guess what!. . . I searched. . . and I found!   And as it turned out, I actually *did* discover a pattern. But it was *not* the pattern I had anticipated, it was something much, much more. . . It totally blew my mind! I discovered not just *one* pattern, but a *whole series* of patterns. . . All of these patterns are inter-related, and they *all* stem from the Three-Way-Connection between; *Alexander - 2300 years -* and the *Six-Day-War* (mentioned earlier, on page 15.) And what's more, is that these patterns dovetail perfectly with the *"Seven Thousand Year Millennial Cycle!"*

The 2300 Year Connection
My First 'Big' Discovery

Out of *all* the quartz samples that I've ever tested (upwards of 3000 samples, and taken from nearly 1000 excursions out in the field) I've found traces of gold at least *one third* of the time. But to see *'visible gold'* right in front of my eyes while digging in a quartz vein. . . I've only seen it 15 or 20 times.

Now, to find *"visible gold"* in a vein, *right at the surface of the ground*, is rarer still. But I found gold in Hawaii! I discovered a rich vein of golden revelation *right at the surface* of the biblical text, in the *old testament book of Daniel!*

It all happened right at the end of the first quarter of the Biblical Studies Course. . . We had been studying the book of Revelation, and the book of Daniel in tandem (because of their similarities.)[14] During that Christmas break, I was reading about one of Daniel's visions, and noticed a profound historical connection about Alexander the Great.

Two hundred years before the days of Alexander, the Jewish Prophet Daniel saw him in a vision. The vision is recorded in the 8th chapter of the book of Daniel. The 'Chapter 8 Vision' began with a scene of the Greeks and their first King (who would be Alexander) conquering the vast Empire of the Medes and Persians (Alexander began this conquest in 334 B.C.)

At the end of the vision, a statement was made concerning the Jewish Temple in Jerusalem. . . "After 2300 evenings and mornings, then shall the Sanctuary be properly restored.." Many have wondered if perhaps the 2300 evenings and mornings here, may refer to a period of time lasting 2300 years. . .

So here's my *big discovery*. . . Here's what I found. . .

(it's on the next page)

During the events of the 1967 Six-Day-War in the Middle East, the ancient site of the Temple Mount in East Jerusalem was *restored* to the Jewish people. . .
To whom it had been lost for more than 2500 years. . .
From the year Alexander began his conquest, until the Six-Day-War, there were exactly 2300 years!

WOW!

You may want to stop and ponder these things for a moment. . . .

I'll wait for you on the next page. . .

The Cornerstone. . .
To An Elaborate System Of Patterns

Soon after this discovery, I realized that the *'2300 Year Connection,'* was only the *'tip-of-the-iceberg*. . . As I studied it more closely, I came to understand that it was the *'cornerstone'* of an elaborate *system* of interconnected patterns in the flow of Western history (the first of which, was the pattern of the *Seven Empires of Western Civilization*. . .)

A Proportional Thing
Two More Interesting Discoveries

Right after I discovered the *'2300 Year Connection,'* I unearthed a couple of *very interesting* things. . .

First, I found that *'2300 years'* is only 33.333 years short of being an exact *'one third'* of 7000 years (2333.333 years = 1/3rd of 7000 years.) That proportion of time (1/3rd of 7000 years), I thought, *may hold* a special numerological significance (from the standpoint of the Millennial Worldview.)

So I simply added 33.333 years to the end of the 2300 years at 1967. . . And *that's* when I began to notice an emerging pattern! It was the *'Pattern of the Seven Empires of Western Civilization.'*

Notice the similarities between the *'2300 Year Connection'* and the *'Pattern of the Seven Empires.'* No doubt, you can see how my discovery of the *'Pattern of the Seven Empires'* was almost a *direct* result of my discovery of the *'2300 Year Connection.'*

(see charts, opposite page)

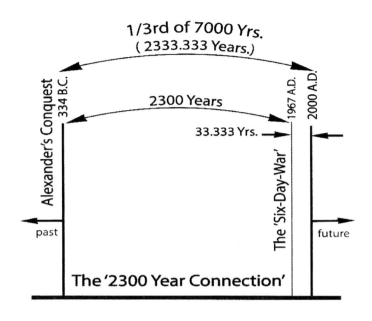

1/3rd of 7000 Yrs.
(2333.333 Years.)

2300 Years

33.333 Yrs.

Alexander's Conquest
334 B.C.

1967 A.D.

2000 A.D.

The 'Six-Day-War'

past

future

The '2300 Year Connection'

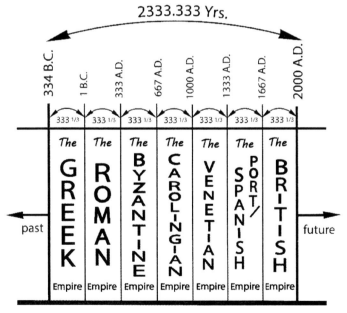

2333.333 Yrs.

334 B.C.   1 B.C.   333 A.D.   667 A.D.   1000 A.D.   1333 A.D.   1667 A.D.   2000 A.D.

333 1/3   333 1/3   333 1/3   333 1/3   333 1/3   333 1/3   333 1/3

The   The   The   The   The   The   The
GREEK   ROMAN   BYZANTINE   CAROLINGIAN   VENETIAN   SPANISH PORT/   BRITISH

past

future

Empire | Empire | Empire | Empire | Empire | Empire | Empire

65

The Second thing I found, was that the proportional difference between *'2300 years'* and *'2333.333 years'* is exactly *'1/70th part'* (another *mathematical* and *numerological* curiosity!)

$$2300.000 \text{ yrs.} = 69 \text{ parts}$$
$$+ \quad 33.333 \text{ yrs.} = 1 \text{ part}$$

$$= \quad 2333.333 \text{ yrs.} = 70 \text{ parts}$$

As we move forward in *"God's Gold!"* I'll explain more about why I added 33.333 years to the 2300 year connection, (page 114.) and also the meaning behind the fascinating 69/70th proportional difference. . .

PART 5

HAPPY

HANUKKAH

Two More Post-Discovery Discoveries
"The Great disappointment Of 1844"
. . . and "Hanukkah"

n the afterglow of my discovery of the '2300 Year Connection' between Alexander the Great, and the Six-Day-War, I began to ask myself a question. . . "How could this be?. . . Why had I never heard of this connection before?"

I began reading all the books I could get my hands on (and I had access to some *pretty good* resources), but I couldn't find any commentaries dealing with this amazing 'three-way-connection.' For a long time, I thought that perhaps I was the only person in the world who had noticed it. . .

But It would be years later, after the development of the "inter-net", that I began to find a small number of others who had made the same '2,300 year connection' as I had. But still, I had to ask the question: "Why was this '2300 Year Connection' not widespread common knowledge among the Millennial Believer's?". . .

I found two main reasons why I believe the *'2300 Year Connection'* has been obscured from the attention of students of Millennial Biblical prophecy.

The *first* reason, is because of a something called: *"The Great Disappointment of 1844"*. . .

The *Second* reason, is because Daniel's chapter 8 Vision appeared to have already been fulfilled around the year 166 B.C. . . . .

Let me give you the background on *both* of these reasons now. . .

Reason #1.
The Great Disappointment
Close! But No Potato. . .

Back in the early 1800's a group of Millennial believers called the Millerites (named such because they were followers of a guy named Miller) were convinced that Jesus was going to return on October 22, 1844. According to Miller, *that date* would signaled the fulfillment of *2300 years* from a very significant date in Israel's past. Miller interpreted Daniel chapter 8 to mean that the *Return of Christ* would take place at the end of the 2300 evenings and mornings (which again, he believed would be fulfilled around the 1844 date). 1844 came and went, but of course Christ never showed up. Many were disappointed. . . *Really* disappointed! That event is now called: *"The Great Disappointment of 1844."*

The *Millerites* were forerunners of the *Seventh day Adventists*. Unfortunately, poor Miller both *mis-calculated and mis-interpreted*. . .   But nevertheless, from the standpoint of *my* apparent discovery, Miller's *'One Day = One Year'* premise seems to have been *right on.*

Miller wasn't the *first* to come up with the '1 day' = '1 year' system of trying to interpret the prophecies of Daniel. In 1830, John Nelson Darby (my relative?) wrote an article in the Christian Herald, which brought forth the idea that; 'Days' can signify 'Years,' in the *Prophetic Language* of the Bible.

Darby is considered to be the *"Father of Modern Dispensationalism."* He was also a modern day pioneer of those trying to understand the *"mystery"* concerning the difference between God's plan of history, as it relates to his Church (primarily Gentile), versus how that same plan relates to the Jewish people.

I would not say that *all* of his conclusions were perfect, but he was definitely a trail-blazing pioneer of those *Modern Millennial Christians* who began to predict a *literal restoration* of the *Kingdom Of Israel* in the Holy Land. I would also assume that Miller was *part* of that *general* following, led by Darby, in as much as Darby seems to have been the first guy (in modern times) to have come up with the Day/Year interpretations Daniel's Prophecies.[15]

Regardless of who first came up with the Day/Year interpretation (getting back to the *"bad call"* by Miller), I would suppose that the initial *"shock"* of the 1844 disappointment may have caused the *'soon after'* students of biblical prophecy, to *shy away* from that particular portion of the Scriptures (Daniel 8.)

Reason #2.
The "Hanukkah" Story
A Struggle Between Greek And Jew

Anybody who knows *anything* about Jewish history, and who reads Daniel's Chapter 8 Vision, would conclude that the vision *and* it's interpretation, perfectly describes the events of something known as: the *Maccabean Revolt*, which took place around 166 B.C. The vision and it's interpretation (which are *both* recorded in Daniel Chapter 8.) describes nearly 180 years of history starting from the days of Alexander, and going *all the way through* to the events of the *Maccabean Revolt.*

The *Revolt* was all about a conflict between the Jewish people and an Evil Greek King named Antiochus IV Epiphanies, who began messing things up in Jerusalem. He defiled the Jewish Temple with the worship of *other gods.* The revolt took place right in the middle of the 333.33 year period of the *first Empire of Western Civilization*, the *Greek Empire.*

Every year around Christmas time, Jewish people celebrate *"Hanukkah",* which is the commemoration of the triumph over Antiochus Epiphanes. Antiochus had instituted (or, backed) a cultural assimilation campaign in Israel which sought to 'Hellenize' the Jewish people. The Hellenist's were essentially trying to turn the Jews into Greeks (in line with Alexander's vision of a *blended world* united by Greek Philosophical and Cultural ideals). It may sound bizarre, but because of cultural embarrassments, some of the Jewish youth of those days (trying to *fit in with the 'Greek' crowd*) were actually undergoing surgical procedures to reverse their circumcision!

At one point in the campaign, the Hellenist's began compelling the traditionalist Jews to sacrifice to Zeus, but a Priest by the name of Mattathias Maccabeus, along with his sons, revolted. Hence, *"the Maccabean Revolt"*. The Greeks took over the Jewish Temple and desecrated it, by setting up an altar in honor of Zeus in the Sanctuary.   upon which they sacrificed swine). By 165 B.C. the Maccabees succeeded against Antiochus. The Temple Sanctuary was re-dedicated, and sacrificial service to the God of Israel were re-instated. A number of Scholars believe that the whole ordeal, no doubt, lasted 2300 days.

If we take into account the disappointment of 1844, as well as the apparent fulfillment of this vision a long time ago, it's no surprise that the Three-Way-Connection has been so grossly overlooked by most Bible Prophecy buffs.

This sign (below) in front of this Seventh day Adventist Church, in my home town of Angels Camp, clearly makes reference to the *"2300 Evening and Morning Vision"* (Daniel Chapter 8:14.) I'm not sure what translation they used, but either way, it is a testifies to the fact that Daniel's chapter 8 vision is still being talked about within the walls of the Seventh day Adventist Church today. . . . At least in Angels Camp!

The sign out in front of the Seventh-day Adventist Church in my home town of Angels Camp. May 5th, 2015.

PART 6

THE

TIMES

OF THE

GENTILES

"Jerusalem"
The City Of God

The restoration of Jerusalem and the Temple Mount site to the Jewish people in 1967 was no small event. It was a *"big deal!"* Not since the very days of Daniel, have the Jewish people (as an autonomous nation) been in control of Jerusalem. Out of all the places mentioned throughout the Bible, the City of Jerusalem is *"The-biggest-deal-place-of-them-all!"* Apparently, everything starts and ends in Jerusalem. Some have even suggested that Jerusalem is actually the same location where Adam and Eve were made. The idea is that Adam was made and then taken to the garden in the east, in Eden. . .

Another tradition tells us that the place where Abraham offered up his son Isaac to be sacrificed was actually the same place in Jerusalem specifically where the Temple came to be located). But regardless of the validity of these theories, the Bible talks a lot about Jerusalem. In fact, the word *"Jerusalem"* is mentioned in the Bible about 800 times. Now take the word *'bread'* for instance, bread is mentioned quite a bit in the Bible, but not as much as Jerusalem.

The word *'bread'* comes in at about 360 times. I hate to say it but Pizza comes in last at 'zero'. I guess it wasn't invented yet? L.O.L! (sorry, tangent. . .)

Before the Israelites entered the land of Canaan to conquer it, the Lord told Moses that a day would come in the nation's future, when he would choose a specific place to put his name ("pitch his tent", "hang his hat", and "settle down" so to speak). In other words, the Lord God of Israel was going to choose a specific place (somewhere in the land of Israel), to set up his platform of worldwide notoriety and fame, in order to draw all mankind towards himself, that they might know him (and his ways). Well, Jerusalem became that *"chosen place."*

And who hasn't heard of his fame? Who hasn't heard of *"Jerusalem,"* and the *"God of Israel"* and all of his *miracles*?

Think about it. . . No doubt, if we mention *"Athens"* (Greece), we probably think of the Greek God's (i.e. Athena, Zeus or Apollo). And if we mention the name; "Cairo" (Egypt), we likely to begin thinking not only of the Pyramids or the Sphinx, but we tend to think of the Egyptian gods like "Isis" or "Ra". But when you think of Jerusalem, you think of the *'Lord'* (the God of Israel). He's pretty famous now, compared to when he first started!

The Bible says that the Lord created the land of Israel to be at the center of all the other nations around her[16]. . . Jerusalem is at the center of the Land of Israel. . . and the Temple Mount is at the center of Jerusalem. Therefore, people throughout history have referred to the land of Israel (and Jerusalem in particular) as; the *'navel,'* or *'belly button'* of the world.

You get the idea, Jerusalem is a pretty important place. So, from a Biblical and historic perspective, the events of 1967 were extremely significant.

Here (above) is my rendition of a 16th century map of the world, created by a guy named Heinrich Bunting. The map shows Jerusalem at the center of the world and joining the three major continents of the *"Old World"* (Europe, Asia, and Africa). The three continents are stylized into the form of a flower or cloverleaf. I love this Map!

The "Times Of The Gentiles"

A History Of The Jews, From Daniel To The Six-Day-War

I n the year 586 B.C., Nebuchadnezzar, King of Babylon, invaded Jerusalem, burned down the Jewish Temple there, and began to rule over the Jewish Kingdom. Thus began an era in Jewish history which the Bible refers to as; *'The Times of The Gentiles.'* The Jewish Prophet Daniel lived during the very days of Nebuchadnezzar, and witnessed the invasion of his homeland by the Babylonian's. He was one of the many Jewish captives who were carted away to become a slave in Babylon. By God's special favor, Daniel was fortunate enough to land a job in the *'Royal Palace'* of Babylon. He became one of the counselors in the court of King Nebuchadnezzar, and he eventually became Nebuchadnezzar's *'chief advisor'*!

The Bible says that the reason the Jewish people lost their Kingdom to the Gentile Nations was because of their disobedience. Moses had given them the rules for success and blessing, but they just wouldn't follow the rules!

In the book of Lamentations (written by the Prophet Jeremiah before the takeover) the lord laments over his people, saying that he only wanted the best for them, he wanted his people to be *'renowned'* (famous) in the eyes of the Gentiles. God's intention for his people, was for them to be an example for all the other nations to follow, but instead they entered into an era of shame. . .

In that year (586 B.C.), after a 2 ½ year long siege, the army of Nebuchadnezzar broke through the walls of Jerusalem, burned down the City and their Temple, then hauled away the people of the land to Babylon to become his slaves. This was the lowest point in the history of the Jewish people up until that time. Thus began a long period of time which came to be known as; *"the times of the gentiles"*.

God revealed to Daniel *'details'* concerning an extended period of time' during which their kingdom would be ruled by foreign kingdoms (*'the Times of the Gentiles'*). Daniel also prophesied (as did other Prophets of Israel) that a time would eventually come, when the kingdom of Israel would again be restored, and be ruled by a *'Great King'*, *'the Righteous One'* who is called; *'the Messiah'*. Daniel pointed out that when that time finally came, the kingdom of Israel (under the leadership of the *'Messiah'*) will rule *the entire world* as well.[17] I guess it goes without being said, that Christianity teaches that *Jesus is the 'Messiah'.*

Post Babylon
The Gentiles Still Rule

Seventy years after the kingdom of Babylon took possession of the city of Jerusalem (and the Jewish Kingdom), the Babylonians *'fell'* to the Medes and Persian's (in one night[18]). Immediately after that transfer of power took place, the Jews were allowed to return to their homeland. The City of Jerusalem and the Temple were re-built! Nevertheless, the Persians still retained authority over the land Israel and the Jewish kingdom.

After 180 years or so, the Persian kingdom was inherited by Greece. Then Greece fell to the Romans (who ended up ruling over Jerusalem with an iron fist). In 70 A.D., the Romans totally destroyed the Jewish Temple, and in the year 114 A.D. they utterly *plowed the City of Jerusalem under.* The Roman's sarcastically re-named the land of Israel *'Palestine',* after Israel's ancient enemies the *'Philistines'.* After *'Rome',* the Byzantines ruled the land. Then the Moslem

Empires etc. for centuries. By the 1800's the Ottoman Empire was ruling supreme over the ancient homeland of the Jews.

"The Zionist's"
And The 'New' Israel

In the 1800's a *'restoration'* began to take place in the land of Palestine. Around 1848 (the same year that the announcement went out that gold had been discovered in California) Jewish people called; *'Zionists'* began immigrating to their ancient homeland (*'Zion'* is simply another name for *'Jerusalem,'* so you might call these Jewish people; *'the Jerusalem-ist's'*!) The *Zionist's* were desiring to create an official *'homeland'* for the Jewish people.

Now to some degree or another, there have probably almost always been at least a few Jewish people living in and around Jerusalem and the ancient land of Israel. They lived under the rule of whatever political power happened to be charge at the time. But for the most part, *'Jews'* (not having a homeland of their own) have been *wandering* from country to country, travelling around throughout the world for centuries. Thus they earned the name; *'the wandering Jews'*.

There was a cycle that seemed to take place wherever they went. The cycle went something like this; At first the Jews tended to be welcome guests in whatever particular country they happened to be living in (or at least tolerated). Then, as time went on, they tended to prosper more than the local natives, who in turn became envious or jealous of their Jewish guests. Inevitably, the natives either *'asked'* or *'demanded'* the Jews to *'pack up'* and *'leave'* their country. This pattern of *'wandering'* became a syndrome.

Apparently, the *'Zionists'* were tired of *'wandering'*, and were hoping to re-claim at least *'some parts'* of their ancient homeland in Palestine. The Zionist's began purchasing parcels of real estate in Palestine, and many proceeded to till the land. The Zionist's also began to plant trees all over the land, for the purposes of shade, and to reduce soil erosion (not to mention that trees are a beautiful addition to the landscape.)

As increasing numbers of Zionist Jews began moving into the Holy Land from around the world, it aroused alarm on the part of many of the local Arabs. As a result, tensions and conflicts have been continuing in the Land of Israel ever since those days. But in spite of struggles and oppositions, the aspirations of the Zionist Jews have consistently been realized throughout the years.

Only a hundred Fifty years ago, the Hebrew language was considered to be a *'dead language,'* but thanks to a man named Ben Yehuda it came back from the dead. Ben began *exclusively* using the language in his own home in Israel, and today, *'Hebrew'* is the common language of the Israeli people. Much more could be said about the amazing transformation of the land of Palestine which is now called Israel, but I'm getting ahead of myself. . . Let's get back to Palestine during the Ottoman's rule. . .

After WWI, everything in the Middle East region changed drastically. The Ottoman Empire (who had allied themselves with Germany) collapsed, and its territories were *'parceled out'* to European countries like France and Great Britain. The British inherited control of Palestine.

The Balfour Declaration
And The 'New Birth' Of A Nation

I n 1917, Great Britain issued a promise to favor and help establish of a National homeland for the Jewish people in Palestine

('The Balfour Declaration'). Immediately, both local and neighboring Arabs began *"making a stink"*, because they didn't like the idea of a Jewish Nation in what was once the Ottoman Empire. One of the reasons for their hostilities was that they viewed a Nation comprised of Jews (predominantly out of Europe) as simply another version of European *Colonialism*, or *Crusade-ism*.

A few years later, the British Government drew up plans for the establishment of a Jewish state (the British Mandate). The borders for other *'Middle Eastern'* States like *Jordan*, *Syria*, *Iran*, and *Iraq* were also drawn up. In 1947, the Zionist's gained independence from Great Britain, and *"officially"* became a *Sovereign Nation* in 1948. But the surrounding Arab countries didn't like the idea of a *'Jewish Nation'* in the region,[19] and began making an even *'Bigger Stink'*! There were military conflicts throughout the 1950's between Arabs and Israelis, and by 1967, five Middle Eastern countries, led by president of Egypt; *'Nasser'* formed an alliance in an effort to completely destroy the Nation of Israel. The Arab League began mounting threats against Israel, threatening to literally *"drive the Israeli's into the Mediterranean"*. The Israeli's were outnumbered by the Arab League, it was a *'David against Goliath'* situation.

The 'Six Day War' officially began around 6 p.m. Sunday evening June 4th 1967 when the Israeli Knesset held a special *'closed session'* meeting and declared war against her enemies, but the fighting began the next morning.

The military action began around dawn on the morning of June 5th 1967. Israeli planes prepared to *take off,* on what would otherwise look like routine patrol flights, but the Israeli planes bombed airfields in Egypt, taking out most of the Egyptians planes. By the end of the day, *All-Out-War* was in progress, but the Israeli's had gained 'air superiority' over their enemies. Victory after victory ensued for the Israeli's. The Arabs cried *'Uncle!',* and the war was over in just *'six days'.*

The Restoration Of The "Lost" Kingdom Of Israel
Jerusalem Restored!

As a result of the 'Six-Day-War,' East Jerusalem, or the *'Old City'* of Jerusalem (which is called; *'the City of David'*) was also *'restored'* to the people of modern day Israel. East Jerusalem was the *'Royal City'* where the King resided; This was the place where King David lived! And the *'Kings house'* was located right next door to the Lord's House (*the 'Temple'*). The *'Temple'* was *'God's house.'* In the 1967 war, both of these places were *'restored'* to jurisdiction and control of Modern day Israel. This was a unique situation for Israel. A situation which had not been seen since before the days of Nebuchadnezzar and Daniel.

Jerusalem does not have a King *'in residence'* at the moment, much less a *'Temple,'* but the general idea in the minds Millennial believer's, is that *things* are being prepared for the return of Jesus Christ (the *'Son of God'* and *'King of Israel,'* A.K.A. the 'Messiah')

FAST-TRACK, BY-PASS TO DISCOVERY > > >
Skip Ahead To Page: 97

The Pathway To Discovery
A hard Road To Travel...

That two year stay in Hawaii was one of the greatest times in my life! But it was one of the hardest and scariest times as well. After two years of married life, my wife Linda,

The Fam! The day we landed on the Big Island

and our 14 month old son Josiah left our home in California, and got on a one way plane to Kona Hawaii with only $20.00 in my pocket. Now, I know this may sound like one of those fantastic

Faith stories, but that's actually the way it went down. . . Twenty bucks! Moving over there the way we did was a real step of faith for us, but it wasn't entirely *'blind faith'*. We actually had a place to stay for a short time (with our friends Ed and Cathy.) They had moved from our hometown area in California to Kailua-Kona a few years earlier, and graciously opened their house to us for a few days in the interim (until we could get *'dialed in'* and moved onto the campus at Y.W.A.M.) The *'twenty bucks thing'* was tough, but we got some cash flow going later on. . . Let me tell you, it's a lot more fun having money and being self-sufficient. Even if you *are* living in Paradise!

Most of the folks at Y.W.A.M. (students, staff etc.) were supported financially (at least in part) through their home church fellowship or friends and relatives. We didn't get a lot of support. . . In fact, some of our support was negative or *'anti-support'*. . . Go figure. . . ':o(.

Somebody suggested that we needed to send *"support letters"* back home to *'let people know'* (or *'remind'* them) about the work we were doing *'out here in the mission field.'* But Hawaii was probably not the ideal place to raise *'support'* from. It didn't sound very much like a *mission field!. . .* Hawaii sounds more like a vacation destination, right?

Anyway, I wasn't really a part of the organization because of a missionary zeal. I was only visiting out there, in order to take some of the courses at the University. Nevertheless, I *did* send out one support letter anyway . . . Not much response. After that, It felt kind of creepy, so I didn't send out anymore '*support letters*'.

Then, there were the support '*phone calls*' *(same idea as the letters, except it was "on the phone")* Using the dormitory pay phone, I tried calling people back home on the mainland. I called a couple of super-rich guys that I knew, to see if I could raise some support from them. One of the two guys (a pretty close friend of mine) was literally worth "*hundreds of millions*," and when I hit him up for some support he told me something like: "*if the Lord is in it, then the Lord will provide the finances.*" Then he told me he would have his secretary send me a check, but nothing ever came, and I never reminded him again. The other *super-rich* dude said he would love to support my stay at a Biblical School, but since YWAM wasn't a Roman Catholic Institution he could not help me. . .

':0 (

Well, I managed to get through those days regardless of a lack of *"ideal"* financial support.

I worked part time jobs, and had my own little *'Lei stand'* for a while, in front of the Kona Inn. I did some *'wheeling-and-dealing'* with a large needlepoint rug that I owned. And at one point, I sold out the royalty rights on my rug designs so I could continue on at YWAM (It was a tough decision, but this is what I was referring to a few pages back (pg.38) when I said; "I believe I had to leave that world behind. . . in order to move into a greater level of discovery.."

All right. . . enough whining and complaining! [not that I was actually complaining, but I was simply trying to point out the fact that oftentimes, when we choose to follow a path of discovery, there can be extremely tough (even bizarre) challenges to face. . . It was tough! And I had my share of *"bizarre"* to deal with as well. Nevertheless, my memories of those days are sweet now. . .] Jesus said the road that leads to LIFE is a tough one to follow, and there are few people who even *"find"* it (Matthew 7:13,14.)

I went out to Hawaii in search of something, and the road to that discovery turned out to be a tough one to follow, but *PRAISE GOD* I found what I was looking for, and even more besides. . .

PART 7

THE

TWO

WAYS

When Worldviews Collide
("Millennialism" vs "A-Millennialism")

During the first three months of the Biblical studies course in Hawaii, we focused on the New Testament of the Bible. The second and third quarters were dedicated to the study of the Old Testament books. We studied each book by reading it over and over 5 times. Then we broke the book up into different levels (i.e. the main theme of the book, the main divisions, then chapters and verses.) We were also challenged to discover the 'one main verse' from the book. That *"one main verse"* was supposed to sum up the main message of that particular book.

We were employing something called; the *"Inductive Bible Study Method"*. It was a really cool way to study the Biblical text, and the teachers produced some great lectures covering things like: the history and development of the *"canon"* of the scriptures, and the historical contexts and backgrounds behind particular books of the Bible etc.

FAST-TRACK, BY-PASS TO DISCOVERY > > >
Continue from here: Read to page 148:

Having fun at Hapuna Beach!

I was having a blast on the Big Island of Hawaii, and going to the school there was great fun! But early on, I was shocked to learn that some (*if not all*) of the '*leadership teaching staff*', did not necessarily hold to the traditional *Millennial* view. But rather, they held to a different view (which sounds confusingly similar) called *"A-Millennialism."* The thinking behind *"A-Millennialism"* just didn't seem quite right to me. And it became quite apparent soon enough, that the two views were completely incompatible with each other. I'll explain all about this, shortly (beginning on page 101.)

Many of my classmates were equally shocked as I, as we listened to instructors teaching the course, who had formerly been, but were now no longer solid Millennial believers! Besides. . . The main reason I came to the Island in the first place was to *'beef up'* my faith in the Millennial view, not to exchange it for something different.

I mean, unless of course, the *other* view was true. . . Could it be? Maybe they knew something that I didn't. . .

The school was fast-paced and intense. We poured over page after page of study and lecture materials, so there wasn't a lot of time for reflection or grappling, if we ran into an unsettling theological issue along the way. This class was *not* for *'babies'*. . . It was like going to a Seminary, and there were *bones* to choke on! And as the days and weeks progressed, I had the feeling that the course was either going to *MAKE* my Faith in Millennialism, or *BREAK* my Faith in Millennialism. Fortunately, what didn't *Kill* my Millennial Faith, made it stronger. In fact, I *won out* victoriously!

Over the next ten pages or so, I'll explain the differences between these two competing worldviews. . .

O.K., . . you can turn to the next page. . .

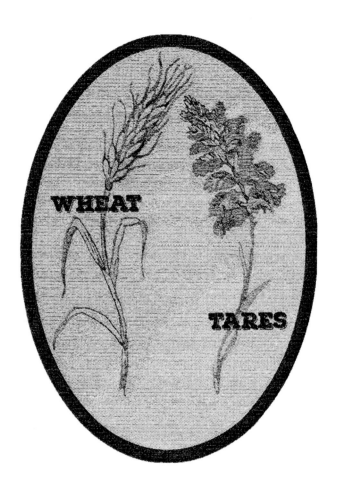

WHEAT

TARES

"Good Seed/Bad Seed"
(The Parable Of The Wheat And Tares)

Jesus told a parable about a farmer who sowed his field with good seed (wheat). But shortly thereafter, an enemy came at night and sowed *tares* (bad seed) into that field. It wasn't discovered until later that there were two different things growing in the same field. The decision was made to let them grow together until harvest time when it would be obvious to tell the difference between the two. The tares could then be carefully taken out of the field without damaging the wheat at the same time (Matthew 24:13-24).

Throughout Church history, two basic teachings have dominated the theological landscape of Christianity.[20] Like the *"Wheat and the Tares,"* these two teachings have produced two different kinds of Christianity. The two have been in competition with each other all throughout church history. The first teaching is the afore mentioned Millennialism. The second teaching (which may sound confusingly similar) is called; A-Millennialism.

The term 'A-Millennial' means *'no'* or *'not'* Millennium. The adherents of the *A-Millennial teaching* don't believe in a *'literal'* thousand year reign of Christ on this earth, much less a seven thousand year cycle of time for the completion of world history. The *A-Millennial teachings* could first be found in the earliest days of the Christian churches. These teachings were simply *'re-definitions'* or *'re-interpretations'* of the elements found in the already existing *Millennial teaching.*

The *A-Millennial teachings* were popularized in the early days of the churches by teachers known as the *'Allegorist's'* (because of the strong use of allegory in their teaching style). The stronghold of the *Allegoristic movement* was based in *Alexandria Egypt*[21] where the Greek influence of *Platonic Philosophy*[22] produced a dualistic view of the universe. In Plato's[23] world *spirit* was considered good and *matter* was considered evil.

You see, the Philosopher *Plato*[23] had combined the *'science'* of the Greek philosophers with the elements of the traditional Greek mystery religions otherwise known as; *Gnosticism.* The Gnostics believed that *matter* was *'evil'* and *spirit* was *'good.'* The *'marriage of ideas'* between the *Greek Science* and *Gnostic Mysticism* created by Plato came to be called *'Platonism.'*[22] The Platonic emphasis on the value of *'spirit'* over *'matter'* was the chief motivation behind the Allegoristic teachings that came out of Alexandria Egypt.

In the minds of the *'Allegorist's,'* all of the promises from God having to do with the *'material world'* were repudiated as being evil. For example, the Old Testament and New Testament promises concerning the *'resurrection of the body'* (matter), and 'Christ's Millennial Kingdom on earth (the material world), even *'time'* itself which is calculated by the movements of the Sun, moon, and stars (the material universe) were all unacceptable conclusions in the minds of the Allegorist's.

Pharos
ALEXANDRIAN LIGHTHOUSE

Here is an illustration I created depicting the great Lighthouse of Alexandria Egypt.
One of the "Seven Wonders of the Ancient World", the 450 foot tall lighthouse produced a beam of light which is believed to have been seen as far as two hundred miles away!

The Allegorist's took all of the elements contained in the *already* established *'Millennial view'* and changed either the nature or meaning of those same elements. For instance, *'one thousand years'* (the time frame of Christ's Millennial Kingdom) no longer meant 1,000 x 365.25 days. Instead, they proposed that it actually means an indeterminably long, long period of time. Again, another example of Allegoristic thought was the proposition that; Christ will not *'literally'* come back to this world, as once believed. Rather, the *Allegorist's* would explain that the *Second Coming of Christ* takes place every time a new believer receives Christ into his heart during the ritual of *baptism*. In this particular view Christ comes into the heart of the believer and conquers the *'world'* of the new believer's bodily desires.

Another allegoristic idea referring to the *'Second Coming of Christ'* suggests, that even if Christ actually *does* return to this world, then the entire nature of the world (*and Universe?*) will suddenly be changed into a *'spiritual'*, *'ethereal'*, or *'heavenly state'* of being (as opposed to a material reality.) The Allegorist's put forth many other *re-definitions* and *re-interpretations* concerning the *'literal'* or *'material'* expectations of those who hold to the *Millennial faith*.

In the New Testament we can find evidence that the Allegoristic teachings were being taught even in the earliest days of the churches.[7] For instance, the book of I Corinthian's revealed a source of confusion that was arising within some of the fellowship groups in Corinth. In his letter to the Corinthians, the Apostle Paul addressed the problem of 'certain troublesome people' who were teaching that Christ had already come, and that the resurrection had already taken place! The Apostle Paul straightened out these issues for the believers there. . . At least for the time being. . .

But eventually, over time, the Allegoristic teachings finally made their way into mainstream Christianity, producing the competing *'Christian Worldview'* which is now known as; *A-Millennialism*.

Now it must be mentioned at this point that there is a difference between the Allegorist's themselves and those who made use of 'allegory' in their teaching. Jesus himself used parables and spoke allegorically to convey truths about spiritual realities[24]. So also, the Apostle Paul. He was a master when it came to the use of *'allegory'* to explain certain mysteries of God's grace[25]. It wasn't the use of *allegory* per se', but rather the *Platonic Greek philosophical influence* and *Gnostic bent* which set the Allegorist's apart from those who taught the tenets of the traditional Millennial Worldview. Over the years there have been *'spin-offs'*[5] [26] and modifications to both steams of Christian teaching. Nevertheless, within the *'field'* of Christianity, there has been essentially only these two views; *'Millennialism'* and 'A-Millennialism'.

Jews Versus Gentiles
Two Different Conclusions

Because of the extreme duality of ideas within Christianity (*'Millennialism'* versus *'A-Millennialism'*), it's not surprising to understand why *'outsiders'* throughout church history (as well as *'insiders'*) have had confusing or conflicting ideas about what *Christians* actually believe. One such case of confusion (coming out of the *'field'* called Christianity) has the question of how *'Gentile'* Christians should view the Jewish people. It looks pretty obvious (from a Biblical perspective) that God has a tender spot in his heart for the descendants of Abraham, Isaac, and Jacob (Israel).

Traditionally, Millennialism has tended to foster a love for the Jewish people, because they are seen as God's uniquely chosen people,[27] through whom He would bless all the nations of the world.[28]

In the New Testament book of Romans the Apostle Paul had *this* to say about the subject; *"to the Jew first, and then to the Greek."*[29] The word *"Greek"* here, in this context, simply meant a *'Gentile'* (anyone who was not a Jew by ethnic descent). Millennialism holds to the belief that God made certain exclusive, unconditional, and irrevocable promises to the descendants of Jacob (Israel), so as to be distinguished from among all other nationalities of the world (the Gentiles).

In short, even if *some* of the Jewish people may have been disciplined by their God because of their unbelief and disobedience towards him, yet God has not (and will not) forsake them utterly.[29, 30]

A-Millennialism on the other hand, has held to a different view of the Jewish people. In their view, Israel (as a genetic race) are no different in the eyes of God than anyone else... After all (the *A-Millennial* thinking goes) God no longer regards *'flesh'* (ethnicity/nationality) as having any significance, because to them *"flesh"* is (in and of itself) a materialistically based *"evil"* thing. And if we add (on top of all this) the fact that the Jews are known for being an exceptionally stubborn and rebellious people (Exodus 32:9),[31] it may be easy to perceive them as being a *"re-eeeally evil"* kind of flesh. . . And *now* you have the makings for a *full scale Jewish Holocaust*!

You can probably see by all of these things, that the two ways of thinking can produce two very different kinds of fruit. Jesus said that you will know them by their fruit. . . Think about that for a while. . .

PART 8

THE

'360' DAY

MYSTERY

Let's Dig A Little Deeper!
The 'Daniel' Vein Produces Pockets of Golden Revelation

J ust like we do, when we discover traces of gold in a quartz vein, I began to dig deeper into the mystery of this *three-way connection* between *Daniel, Alexander,* and *the Six-Day-War.* . .

Now even though I found a direct connection with '2,300 years,' I was still curious to understand the numerological meaning behind the number 2,300. I mean, why did it take 2,300 years for the Vision to be fulfilled, as opposed to any other number of years, like, say; "2,200," or "2,400," or even something like 777 years?

For centuries, students of this passage have speculated and wondered what the actual number (*2,300*) means. It seems as though *all* of the symbolic numbers, mentioned in the Bible, are connected to the number seven, in some way or another.

I'll give you an example of what I mean. In the book of Revelation there is a reference to the number *"1,260"* (Revelation 11:3). So is 1260 connected to the number seven. . . ?

At first glance, It may not look like 1,260 is related to the number seven, but I'll tell you right now, that 1,260 is *definitely* related! Here's how:

As it turns out, 1,260 days is exactly *one half* of a *seven year period*, whose years are composed of 360 days (360x7 = 2,520 x 1/2 = 1,260!) The *'360 day year'* is a big topic, and we'll be talking about *it* a little later on. But you see, the number *'seven'* (or derivatives of it) show up *all over the place* in the Bible!

At any rate, I began to *search* for the numerological meaning of 2300, and after a bit of digging, I found! I discovered yet another pocket of gold in the *"Daniel Vein"*! I discovered the unique numerological significance behind the number 2300! It all came in *three* stages! Here's how it went down. . .

[Now actually, I already went over the first two stages of this discovery back on pages 64-66. but I'll go over it again anyway (It may be good at this point to refresh your memory a bit.)]

Stage 1. First, I saw something glimmering in the *Daniel Vein*, and I knew that it was *definitely* gold! It was a *clue* about the number 2,300. . .

I noticed that 2,300 years is only 33.333 years short of being a perfect *'third'* of *seven thousand years*. In other words, 1/3rd of the entire *7,000 year Millennial cycle!* (which would seem to hold special numerological significance in light of the Millennial teaching.)

Stage 2. After digging a little deeper, I found another eye opening display of glory. . . A clue, which seemed to confirm that the *previous one* was on track. I noticed that the difference between 2,300 years, and 2,333.333 years is exactly 1/70th part (see page 66.) So if we add 33.333 years to the '2,300 years,' the *new* period extends out, to the year 2000, and equals exactly 1/3rd of 7000 years.

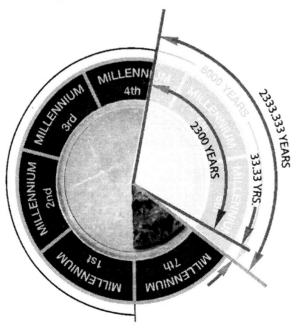

Stage 3. At *this* point in the search, I wondered if my quest to prove a *'Solid Numerological Connection'* between *"2300 years,"* and *"a proportion of time equaling "1/3ʳᵈ of 7000 years,"* may only be conjecture, or wishful thinking. But I kept digging for truth. . .

And as I hammered and chiseled my way deeper into the revelation of the *"Daniel vein,"* I finally broke into a major pocket of *'Solid Gold Truth!'*

I discovered an unusual *link* between the standard *'365.25 day year,'* and a special *'360 day long year.'* This *'link'* in turn produced a *'Solid Connection'* between the *'2300 years'* and *'a perfect proportion of "one-third" of 7000 years!'* The key is *all about* the *'360 day'* year. . .

[Now, I just may have lost you, with all of those numbers, and my many words. But try to hang in there, and you'll see what I'm talking about soon enough. First, let's go over a little background info about the origins of the special *"360 day year,"* and why it is important. Then, I'll show you the *'Solid Gold Revelation of Truth'* which ties together *'2300 years'* with the *'7000 year Millennial Cycle. . .'*]

Time As We Know It
The '360' Day Year

One *'Calendar'* year is roughly 365.25 days in length, but the Apostle John (author of the book of Revelation) alluded to a certain type of year that consists of *'360 days'* (with *'months'* that are exactly thirty days in length). This special type of year has been referred to as; the *'Prophetic Year'* or *'Holy Year'*. But maybe we should just call it; *'John's Year'*!

So where did the Apostle John come up with this *'360 day year'* anyway? Apparently it came to him by prophetic revelation (I mean, hey. . . they didn't call it the book of *Revelation* for nothing!) All joking aside, some critics assert that John was simply an uneducated man, and that he actually believed that there were only *360 days* in a year, and *thirty days* in a month. Hogwash! Anyone can count the days of a month, or even a year for that matter! Especially a first century Jew, who was keenly aware of the many complicated feast days in the Jewish calendar.

But there is *one* theory about the origin of the 360 day year that makes really good sense to me. The Theory takes in to account, the biblical story of the great flood that happened in the days of Noah. It goes like this:

In the beginning, at the creation of the world, the original *'calendar year'* was 360 days. The earth was closer to the sun making the overall ambient temperature of the atmosphere much warmer than it is now. Because the earth was closer to the sun it had a faster orbit (360 days). Because of the earth's closer position to the sun, solar heat produced *way more* water vapor at higher levels in the upper atmosphere than presently. These vapors produced a *'greenhouse effect'* making the earth a wonderful place to live.

Also, the water vapor in the upper atmosphere shielded the inhabitants of this world from many of the harmful forms of solar and cosmic radiation. This could be one reason why people lived much longer in those days (upwards of 900 years).

The Bible paints a picture of the world (before the flood) in which there was no rain, and no extreme heat or cold. The account seems to suggest, that clothing was not even necessary for warmth during those times. But during the days of Noah, planet 'X'[67] (located between Mars and Jupiter)[67] exploded, thus leaving behind the present day asteroid belt.[67] A massive chunk of planet 'X' (or a huge meteor) struck the earth near what is now the Yucatan peninsula around present day Mexico. The Meteor knocked the earth out to a larger orbit, farther away from the sun, where it suddenly became colder. Then, the huge volume of water vapor stored in the upper atmosphere began to condense into rain (40 days and nights worth!)

Flooding began, ice caps formed, and a worldwide catastrophe ensued. Because of the meteoric blow, the Earth became tilted on its axis' thus producing yearly seasonal changes, which (according to the biblical account) began just after Noah's flood.

Because of the Earths new distance *farther away* from the sun, a slower orbit was established, which is the present *365.25 day* orbit.

Wow! What a theory huh? Perhaps it's true. But either way, regardless of the validity of this theory, John refers a 360 day year in the Book of Revelation nonetheless (see Revelation 11:i.e. 1,260 days).

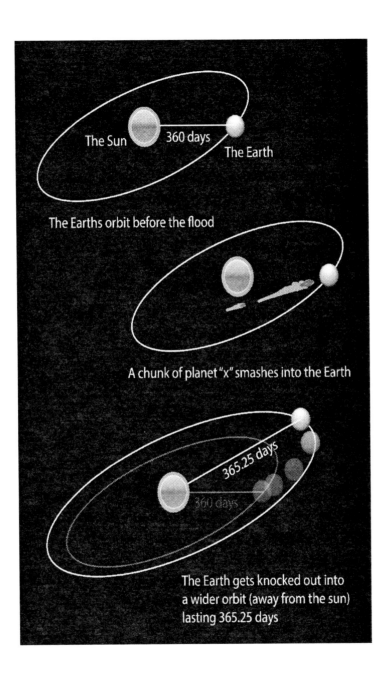

The Earths orbit before the flood

A chunk of planet "x" smashes into the Earth

The Earth gets knocked out into a wider orbit (away from the sun) lasting 365.25 days

The Stage 3. Pocket of Solid Gold Truth

"The '2300 years'= '1/3ʳᵈ of 7000 Years'

So *here's* how it works with the *'360 day year'*. . . When we introduce the shorter (*360 day*) cycle of years into the timeframe of 2300 *'Regular Calendar'* years (365.25 day), then 2,300 *'Calendar'* years becomes 2333.333 years! That's exactly *1/3ʳᵈ of the 7000 year Millennial Cycle* (2,333.333 years)!

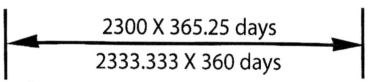

$$\text{2300 X 365.25 days}$$
$$\text{2333.333 X 360 days}$$

These two timeframes equalize, within the same year. There's only a '75 day' difference, in over 840,000 days!

Wow! That definitely looks like more than just a coincidence doesn't it! And it gets better. . . The *next* pocket of *"God's gold"* on the *Daniel Vein* was huge. . . It was the pattern of the *"Seven Empires,"* and it's coming up next, in PART 9. . .

PART 9

THE

PATTERNS

"The Mystery Of History"
Explained!

When I was a kid in school, looking at history was, well. . . like looking at a big pot of stew! Everything was mixed together. I had a hard time figuring out *who* went *where* on the timeline of history. I don't know if it was just my imagination, but it seemed like the schools I went to, focused more on teaching courses called *"social studies"* and *"current events,"* than on teaching a comprehensive system of understanding the last two thousand years of world history.

All the kids I knew growing up (mainly boys) made believe they were Pirates, Roman soldiers, or Medieval knights (with the help of garbage can lids for armor.) But no one actually had a real good grasp on how these historical characters fit together with one another chronologically.

Well. . . This next big *'Pocket of Gold'* that I discovered in the *"Daniel Vein"* pulls all things together in Western history, from Alexander to the present day. It not only puts everything together chronologically, but also reveals that the *flow of Western History* has been following a *pre-ordained* path to a *pre-determined* destination. It reveals an amazing *"Blueprint"* or *"Scheme"* behind *all* of the events of Western History.

"Alexander the Greek"
The Founder of Western Civilization

Let's imagine we are about to watch a film. We've got our popcorn, and a drink. . . The film is about to start. It's an epic style docudrama about the life and times of Alexander the Great. The movie is called: *"ALEXANDER THE GREAT, Founder Of Western Civilization".*

The film begins with a curious image of the Egyptian Sphinx, windblown, and partially covered in bleach blonde desert sand. As we gaze… transfixed by the appearance of this mysterious monument from antiquity we can hear the faint sounds of a breezy wind blowing (drowned out only by the crunching sounds of popcorn on our inner ears).

Then, the narrators voice comes through and gently seizes our attention. The style and sound of his voice is remarkably similar to that of Charleston Hesston. *"History is a deep subject"* he says,. . . *"the deepest well in the desert of human existence. . . We lengthen the cords, that we may draw even deeper, the waters of life that come from understanding our past".* . . We can tell right now, that this is going to be a *"really cool"* movie!

Next, the scenery and mood changes, and we appear to be somewhere in the Mediterranean countryside of Greece. . .

It's like, a perfect spring day (about sixty six degrees and sunny). And now it's as if we are actually right there inside the movie! A few small clusters of white cumulus clouds glisten with their proverbial *'silver linings'* as they drift nearly motionless against the brilliant blue sky overlooking the Greek landscape. The faint smell of Mediterranean Cyprus can be detected amongst a quiet symphony of other fragrances sailing along in the morning breeze.

The *'Mediterranean Cyprus'* are those trees that grow straight up towards the sky like pillars. They look like the heads of enormous spears jutting upwards as if they were defiantly taunting the very heavens. Like soldiers, they march serenely across the stone strewn landscape of this ancient Greek world. The year is 334 B.C.

Breaking the relative silence of the morning, a *'rush of doves'* flies overhead. They've been routed from their place of peace by unfamiliar noises coming just over the hill from the west. The sound crescendos to a muffled roar. It's the sound of men walking, people talking, horses, wagons, and the clatter of metal jangling. Suddenly they appear! An enormous armored throng, moving into the low-lying areas. They roll in like a flood. Before long the valley is brimming with burnished bronze, leather strappings, and the lean muscle of men and horses.

It's an epic scene. It's the army of Alexander of Macedon, later to be known as; 'Alexander the Great'. He and his army are on a grand military expedition to overthrow the sprawling Persian Empire in the east. Just two years earlier, Alexander became *'King of Macedonia'* in place of his father Phillip, who had been assassinated by poisoning. No doubt Olympia participated in the plot. Olympia was Philips first wife, and the mother of Alexander.

You see, Phillip had been taking to himself a number of other wives and these were bearing children to him. Apparently the motive behind Olympia's involvement in the assassination plot was that she feared one of the children from Phillips 'other wives' would inherit the throne instead of her son Alex---------

Pause!

For thousands of years, the story of *Alexander the Great* has been told and re-told. Alexander is known the world over for his military conquests, and the legacy of the vast Empire he created.

The details of his life and exploits are some of the most well documented of any other person in history. Tons of movies have been made, and volumes of books have been written about him. But let's just *'fast forward'* for a moment and take a look at some of the highlights of Alexander's career, as well as the profound impact that he made in the world by the things he set in motion.

In a short 6.4 years (about 2300 days) Alexander succeeded in overthrowing the entire Persian Empire (which had stretched all the way from Turkey to India). After he conquered the Persian Empire, He set up shop in Babylon and celebrated his victories. After partying hard for a couple of years he set his sights south and began making preparations to take the Arabian

Peninsula, but before the campaign started his life suddenly ended (presumably from a mosquito bite).

Alexander's
"One World Order"
Through the Alexandrian Cities

A lexander's zeal to conquer would not have been quenched even if he had taken Arabia, for *his* was a vision of *'Total World Domination.'* He dreamed of establishing a *'One World Order'*. . . a *'Brotherhood of Man'* which would be united by the 'enlightened' ideals of the Greek philosophers.

As a young boy, Alexander was taught the *"Way"* of the Greek Philosopher's. In fact, his personal tutor was none other than Aristotle, the greatest Greek Philosopher of them all! In Alexander's mind he was convinced that the *"Greek Way"* was the *"Best Way. . .* And he was eager to spread the *good news* of the *"Greek Way"* to the ends of the earth!

As Alexander conquered, he established Greek cities along the way. All of the cities bore the name; *"Alexandria".* The *Alexandrian Cities* were scattered everywhere throughout the vast new

Empire created by young Alexander. The most notable of them was *"Alexandria Egypt"*.

The purpose behind the Alexandrian cities was brilliant. They were for the promotion and propagation of the Greek culture. They would become the *"glue"* for Alexander's *"One World Order"*. The vast new territories that Alexander had conquered consisted of varying and diverse people groups, but the *Alexandrian Cities* offered a unification of culture. . .

A new and better way. . .

The *"Greek Way!"* [32]

Well. . . The *Alexandrian Cities* actually worked. Pretty soon, people from Europe, all the way to India, began thinking and acting like Greeks! Following their establishment, the Alexandrian Cities kept on churning out the *Spirit of Greek Culture* for centuries, regardless of which successive *Western Political System* happened to be ruling. . . Consequently, the *'Greek Way'* has been handed down to each successive generation, throughout *all* of Western History.

The Seven Empires
Through the Alexandrian Cities

Now, if we stand back, and take a look at the *'big picture'* of western history from the days of Alexander until the present, we will find that seven great empires have ruled the Western World in an unbroken succession. Again, the lineup goes like this;

1. The Greeks...

2. The Romans...

3. The Byzantines...

4. The Carolingians (*Charlemagne's family line*)...

5. The Venetians, (*the Crusader period*)...

6. The *Dual Empire* of the Portuguese and Spanish...

7. The British Empire.

The Pattern

The first Empire in the lineup was Greece, which we are going to say "officially began" when Alexander began his conquest in the year 334 B.C.[59] So, from midsummer of that year, until *'New Year's Eve'* of the year 1 B.C. there were exactly 333.333 years.

Now, in that year, (1 B.C.), Caesar Augustus was reigning supreme in Rome. Augustus was the *very first* Roman Emperor. And over the next three centuries, a succession of *other* Caesars followed in his footsteps. . . .

Then, 333.333 years later, in the year 333 A.D., we find a unique Roman Emperor named *Constantine* reigning. Constantine was a whole new kind of Roman Emperor, he was a *'Christian'*. Constantine was probably best known for making Christianity *'legal'* in the Roman World. But he did much more than that, he laid the foundations for an entirely *New Empire*, a uniquely *'Christian'* Empire.

Constantine established the headquarters (for what was to become this *third* great empire of Western Civilization) at the site of an ancient city called; Byzantium (where *East* met *West*) in what is now modern day Turkey. *Byzantium* was strategically located at the Bosphorus Strait, which is a *sea river* that connects the Black Sea to the Sea of Marmara (which in turn connects with the Aegean, and subsequently to the Mediterranean Seas) It is also the natural geographical dividing place between the Continents of Europe and Asia Minor.

This area of the World was sort of like a *Crosshairs Region*. Where, on the one hand, vital seaways run *North and South*, and on the other hand, a natural *Land Route* travelling *East and West* between the two Continents. This was the crucial area that Alexander had to break through, when he began to establish his campaign to conquer *all* of the Asian Continent.

The name of the City (Byzantium) was changed to Constantinople (after Constantine). Constantine's Empire later came to be known as; the *Byzantine Empire*. By the way, our present *Christian Calendar System*, which begins on the year 1. A.D., was first put into place during the days of the Byzantine Empire.

Around the middle part of the seventh century the size and influence of the Byzantine Empire became suddenly, and drastically reduced as a result of Arab/Mohammedan invasions. But it was precisely during this time, that the *fourth Great Empire of Western Civilization* began to rise out of obscurity from the central area of Western Europe; "The Carolingian Empire."

Now the glory days of the Byzantine Empire lasted for about. . .

. . . You guessed it. . . 333.33 years!

This amazing 333.33 year pattern (see chart on opposite page) has repeated throughout the entire history of Western Civilization marking the *"rise and fall"* of every one of the *"Seven Great Empires of Western Civilization"*. . . . . Wow!

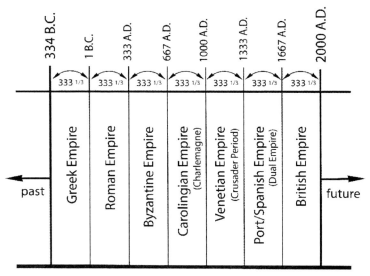

The Seven Empires of Western Civilization

Just as a side note, there is another fascinating point of interest, which applies to *all* of the Seven Empires. Each empire was marked by their very own unique style of architecture. . . .

O.K. . . Let's keep going. . .

The fourth Empire, the Carolingian, was ruled by a royal family blood line of which Charlemagne was a member. They ruled over the larger areas of central Europe. Germany, Italy, and especially the French areas. The Carolingians were the *Crucial Element* that

Charlemagne

resisted the *Moslem Scourge* (the Moors) from enveloping the European Continent.

Charlemagne's Grandfather, '*Charles Martel*', defeated the Moors. The name; *"Martel"* was a name that he earned, in French it means *"The Hammer"*. And like a hammer, in the hand of the Christian God, he hammered out the terrible threat of the Moslem invaders around 732 A.D.

The Carolingian bloodline continued for centuries. But the last vestiges of the Carolingian Monarchs finally disappeared in around the year A.D. 1000 with the death of Louis V in 987 A.D. Louis V, called; *"the Sluggard"*. He was one of the great, great, (etc.) grandsons of Charlemagne. . .

Again, The Carolingian Empire lasted a total of approximately (if not exactly!) 333.333 years! Charlemagne himself lived and reigned around the apex of the Empire. His rule brought about *huge* social, political, and religious changes to Europe. In many ways his political career was very similar to that of Alexander the Great[33].

The *fifth Great Empire of Western Civilization* was that of the *Venetians*. The Venetian Empire was actually a result of the *Crusader Movement*. By the year 1000 A.D. tensions were escalating between *Western Christendom* and *the Churches of the East*, but the common enemy of *both* were the *Persian/Moslem* entities who controlled access to Holy sites in Palestine and Jerusalem.

In the earliest years just after the year 1000, the Egyptian Fatimid Caliph, *"Al-Hakim bi-Amr Allah"* (known as; The *"Mad Caliph"*) ruled over Jerusalem and Palestine. He began persecuting Christians (and Christian pilgrims) in Jerusalem and the Holy Land. In 1004 he forbid the celebration of Easter, and as the years went on, he ordered the destruction of all Christian Churches.

This really *screwed things up* in the Holy Land, for the better part of the first half of the eleventh century. And by the year 1095 the tensions between Christian and Muslim lead to the first Crusade to liberate Jerusalem and the Holy Land from Muslim control. The Crusaders sought to put control the *Holy Land* and especially the ancient *City of Jerusalem* into the hands of Western Christendom. The *City of Venice* became instrumental for the transport of people and supplies to the Middle East during the Crusader Period. This activity *went on* throughout most of the *fifth* 333.333 year period (1000 A.D. to 1334 A.D.) During the Crusader Period, the Venetians established strongholds and trading posts in various places around the Mediterranean lands and coastlines.

By the 1300's the Venetians held a virtual monopoly on trade throughout the entire Mediterranean region. The use of the magnetic compass helped double the capabilities of the Venetians commercial transports. Tons of spices from the far east and Indies came *'Via-Venetia'*, but things began to change radically for the Venetians when the Portuguese and Spanish began *'by-passing'* the Mediterranean trading routes. They started sailing around the horn of Africa in order to trade directly with the Indies. Thus began the *'Sixth' Great Empire of Western*

Civilization (which was actually a *'dual'* empire): "The Port/ Spanish Empire".

L ooking back over Western History, from Alexander's day until the present times, one can see that the expansion and sphere of influence of Western Civilization has grown ever larger with the advent of each new empire. This expansion was especially evident during the times of the dual empire of the Portuguese and Spanish (A.D.1333 – A.D.1666).

Henry the Navigator (a Portuguese Prince) led the way down the unexplored coast of West Africa. These bold exploratory moves eventually resulted in the establishment of a sailing route around the African continent to the Indies. About mid-way into this *Sixth* 333.33 year period (A.D.1500), began the rise of the Spanish Explorers. Columbus was to the Spanish, what Henry the Navigator was to the Portuguese. He of course led the Spanish *West* in search of yet *another* route to the Indies. A Portuguese was actually the first to finally make it west to the Indies, but Columbus accidentally found something even better. . . He discovered a *Whole New World*, the *'Americas'*!

Shortly after Columbus' discovery of the New World, the Portuguese circumnavigated the globe, and began charting out the entire Western

Hemisphere. The lands of the Western Hemisphere soon became a *power grab* between the Portuguese and Spanish. So in order to keep peace, the leaders of these two kingdoms went to see the Pope in Rome in order to get counsel in regard to territorial claims in the new world. The Pope drew a line dividing the *New World* in half. He gave *one half* to the Portuguese and the *other half* to the Spanish. Overall, the Spanish ended up becoming the *greater* of the two.

By the late 1500's the English had become a threat to Spain. So much so, that the Spanish sent their entire Armada (navy) up to take over England. Unfortunately for the Spanish, the Armada was destroyed by a storm at sea in the year 1588. The destruction of the Spanish Armada greatly diminished the influence and power of Spain (to say the least!). England was left to fill the power vacuum left by the Spanish. During this time England was eager to get *'a piece of the action'* in the new world, so they established colonies on the eastern seaboard of North America. By 1666 the British had become Lords of the open seas.

Now there's something to say about the particular year of 1666. It was the first year to be called; *"Annus Mirabilis"*, meaning *"year of* miracles", because it was *A Miracle* that England could have survived through that year, seeing all of the things she faced. She survived wars against the Dutch, to a fire in London, that burned down 13,000 buildings, yet the people who perished in the fire were less than could be counted on both hands. *That* was a miracle! Also, in the beginning of that year, *the Great Plague of London* finally subsided. Now when you think of a Miracle, you tend to think of only positives.

But England's *'year of 1666'* was more of a *miraculous survival* through a *trial by fire*. Sort of like the three friends of Daniel, who were thrown into the fiery furnace by Nebuchadnezzar. But they escaped un-harmed. Remember the principal that each Empire had their own unique architecture? Well, after the 1666 fire in London, the City was re-built in a totally new Architectural style. Thus, with a unique *bang*, started the *"Seventh"* great empire of Western Civilization, 'Great Britain'.

The British Empire went *'over the top'* and became the first *truly* global empire. It was said that; *"the sun never sets on the British Empire"*. By 1834 (the middle of the seventh 333.333 year period), British Colonies could be found practically everywhere, in just about every *'time* zone.' As a matter of fact, I believe the *'time zones'* themselves were invented by the British!

British Industrialization
A World Changing Phenomenon

t would be virtually impossible to overstate the profound impact brought upon the world by the phenomenon called; 'The Industrial Revolution'. And it must said here, that it all started in *'Merry Olde England,'* the homeland and headquarters of the *"Seventh Empire"* of Western Civilization, the British Empire!

Nevertheless, the glory that was Great Britain has diminished considerably. In the year 2000 the Queen of England had to start paying personal income taxes... What!? Kings and Queens collect taxes from their subjects, not the other way around! If that wasn't a *death blow* to a kingdom and an Empire, what would be!

A Maccabean Surprise!

Let's jump back for a moment to the first empire (the Greek Empire). There's a side pocket of gold that we missed... Actually, the "Daniel Vein" sort of branches off in a different direction right here. In hard rock mining it's called a "stringer vein" There's more to this thing than meets the eye... An intriguing numerological surprise pops up within the this 333.33 year period in relation to the Maccabean era. Take a look at the segment from the chart that we looked at earlier (below). The events of the Maccabean era took place precisely during the middle of the first (Greek) Empire! I'll have more to say about this at another time,[34] but notice the proportional element connecting the events around 166 B.C. in relation to both Alexander and the rest of this "Mystery of Western History."

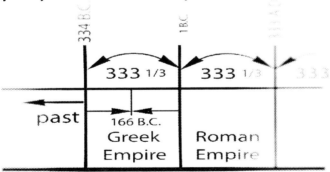

The Seven Empires of Western Civilization

"Globalization"
The Big "G"

Even though the Portuguese and Spanish explorations uncovered a whole new world, the world at large became a much *'smaller'* place. And as a result of British colonization, certain parts of the earth (which in times past were only known through unsubstantiated myths and legends) were now charted out on global maps. Travel to such *'far flung'* places became commonplace for many British travelers and sailors.

Now, it's obvious that the British were *'big'* on colonization, they were the undisputed leaders of their respective times. Nevertheless, they were not the *only* Western Europeans to venture out onto the 'open seas' and claim lands for their King or Queen. Altogether though, and in competition with one another, Western Europeans essentially colonized the entire world!

Through the European colonial movement all the inhabitants of the world were introduced to Western social and technological advances (many of which no doubt were looked upon by many a native people as magic at best). And through the Colonial system (having previously been established) advances in communication, along with the fruits of industrialization, new levels of prosperity began to flood the entire world. Railroads were built across deserted areas which were previously either impossible or at least impracticable for commercial travel.

"Democratization"
Anti-Imperialism & Anti-Colonialism

As the torrent of British and European colonization spread throughout the earth, it was followed *'at the heels'* by a world-wide Anti-Imperial/Anti-Colonial movement based upon Greek ideals of Democratic government.

The formation of the U.S.A. was a prime example of this movement. Not only was there a spreading of Western culture by means of the seven empires individually, but a worldwide political and philosophical unification of sorts (the roots of which were uniquely Greek) began coming to the forefront in every place that bore the mark of Western Man's footprint. By the mid 1900's the movement towards World Democratization resulted in the formation of a global government called the 'United Nations'. The rest is history.

O.K. . . You get the picture. All of these things are without question a *'big deal'*. These political events have re-shaped the very fabric of our entire world, and in no subtle means either. No, these things have been branded upon the face of this world's consciousness. . . 'Western Man' has effectively conquered the world. . . And it all started with Alexander and his vision of Total World Domination.

The Seven Empires, over a period
of time lasting 1/3rd of 7000 years!

What an amazing phenomenon of history!

Again, you may want to stop and ponder these things for a moment..............

Go ahead, take your time. . . I'm not going anywhere. .

What An Amazing Pattern
Very Revealing!

Without a doubt, this is an amazing pattern. It puts all of Western History into perspective as well as revealing the path of global conquest by Western Man.

The fact that the pattern equals 1/3rd of 7000 years seems to *back up* the idea that there actually *is* a 7000 year cycle! And the fact that the pattern converges at the *end* of the Sixth Millennium, seems to imply that *this* is the time around which Jesus is expected to return.

HALF

TIME!

FAST-TRACK, BY-PASS TO DISCOVERY > > >
Skip Ahead. . .Go To Page 184:

Well, we've now made it about half-way through *"God's Gold!"* and if this were a football game, we would be watching the *Half Time Show* right now. . . So how do you like it so far???

Now is the time to raid the fridge! Maybe you should go make a sandwich or something. . . And hey! You might even get lucky and find a piece of pizza left over from the night before!

[I'm not going to try to fool you, this next part is nothing but a shameless *"plug"* for my home town! It will probably sound more like a tourist & travel advertisement than anything else. But this stage in our journey, you *may* enjoy a little visit to *Small Town America*! On the other hand, if you'd rather skip this commercial, then FAST-FORWARD past Angels Camp, and meet me at the beginning of PART 11, on page 161.]

ANGELS CAMP CALIFORNIA

My Town!
A place of Discovery

was born in a small town!. . .
Hey, that sounded like a mid-80's *John Cougar Mellencamp* song didn't it? Yea, it's one of my favorites. . . Anyway, I was born and raised in a small town. . . Even found Jesus in a small town! When I first heard that song I thought 'for sure' he was singing about my town! Now nothing against the hometown of John Mellencamp, but Angels Camp is *"extra special."* At least I'd like to think it is. LOL!

Angels Camp is a small town with a big history. I hope you'll bear with me whilst I indulge in a little boasting about my hometown. I want to share with you some of our local treasure and history.

Angels Camp is strategically located in the heart of California's Mother Lode Gold Country on highway 49. The highway is named after the 1849 Gold Rush. The present day highway was originally a trail that connected all the mining towns that sprang up along the Mother Lode Quartz vein. Like a solid wall of quartz rock, the Mother Lode Vein literally spans a 200 mile stretch (4 hours) of highway 49. The vein travels from Oakhurst to the south all the way up to the City of Grass Valley at its northern end!

Angels Camp falls literally (almost precisely) at the center of the stretch! In 1853, the largest gold nugget in the world (at the time) was discovered just 3 ½ miles from Angels Camp, in our satellite community of Carson Hill. The Carson Hill Gold specimen weighed 195 pounds. Out of all the largest gold specimens found in the world, the Carson Hill nugget was the most unique, because it was formed in the shape of a great big golden staff, or walking stick.

Also at Carson Hill, a unique mineral compound called a *"gold telluride"* was discovered in 1861. The unusual mineral was given the name *"Calaverite"* (after Calaveras county) seven years after its discovery. It would be difficult for me to explain to you exactly *what Calaverite* is, other than that it composed partly of gold and silver but is *very rare* and I would *love* to find a specimen of it myself! I actually found signs of *Telurides* at the hillside mine!

Aside from stories of gold and minerals, Angels Camp and its surrounding vicinities have a lot to brag about. We've all heard of the Golden Gate Bridge haven't we? Well, the concrete used to construct the bridge was made less than ten miles from Angels Camp at the *Calaveras Cement Co*.

Now, if we were to make Angels Camp the epicenter and measure out from there, we will discover all kinds of cool things. . . For instance, Talk about a discovery. . . Only 18 miles from Downtown Angels (as the crow flies) the very first Giant Sequoia tree was discovered. The *"discovery tree"* was felled the same year that the Carson Hill nugget was discovered. The tree was around 1200 years old when it was cut down in 1853. That means the Discovery tree was not much more than a sapling just before the Moslem scourge hit the world during the last days of the Byzantine Empire (find it on the chart of Seven Empires). . . The diameter of the tree was about 24 feet! Today you can go up and sit on the stump of the *"Discovery tree"* at the *"California Big Trees State Park."*

Another little known *world record phenomenon* is just up the road from Big Trees in the town of Dorrington. Right beside Hwy. 4, just behind the Dorrington Hotel, stood the largest *Sugar Pine* tree in the entire world! I understand that only recently, they had to cut the old tree down, but you can stop in and still see the stump.

Next, only fifty seven miles from Angels Camp, you will find the magnificent Yosemite Valley. The Valley is home to the tallest waterfall in the United States. The Yosemite Falls is a whopping 2425 ft. That's almost half a mile high! And it's only 25% shorter than the tallest waterfall in the entire world (Angel Falls in Venezuela.) Every year roughly one million visitors *"discover"* Yosemite for the very first time.

By-the-way, one of my ancestors (my Grandfathers Grandfather, Andrew Davidson Firebaugh) was one of the *first-people-ever* to see El Capitan and the Yosemite Valley! Obviously, the local Yosemite Indians were there first, but we're talking about *"Western Man"* here. . .

According to the story that I heard, Andrew was with a company of soldiers chasing Indians who had been stealing horses and eating them. Back then the horses were like cars. . . Some were more valuable than others (there are really nice cars, and junky cars), so when the Indians began stealing the *Mercedes* and *Rolls Royce's* of the Equestrian World (and bringing them home for their bar-b-que dinners. . .) Well, something had to be done. . . They followed the horse thieves over the top of El Capitan, and were stunned by the beautiful Yosemite Valley!

O. K. . . Here's another one for the record books. In the month of January 1911 in Tamarack California 32 feet of snow fell (the most ever recorded in a calendar month). At the end of that winter Tamarack measured the world's record snow depth of 38 feet! All of this *"Winter Weather"* took place less than 43 miles from Angels Camp.

Frog Town!
Where The Frogs Jump

I must tell you one more most unusual thing about my home town. There's a yearly celebration in Angels Camp which been going on for some time now. . . It's called *"The Frog Jump."* Every year, during the third weekend in

May, you can compete in the frog jumping contest at the *"Calaveras County Fair & Jumping Frog Jubilee."* The festivities take place at *"Frog Town,"* (which is actually the County Fairgrounds) located just outside of the town towards Carson Hill. *'Angels Camp'* and *'frogs'* have found themselves a peculiar and inseparable match, especially over the past eighty seven years! It all started with Mark Twain[35] *("King of Irreverence," "Champion of Humanism"*. . . And a major forerunner of *"Global Liberalism"*).

In 1865 Mark Twain heard a story at the Angels Hotel, about two guys gambling on a race between a couple of frogs! He published a version of the story and it became the propelling agent that launched his literary career. So, Mark Twain's launching pad was actually a lily pad from Angels Camp! In 1928 the City celebrated the paving of its Main Street with an *"all day festival"* centered around a *"Gold Rush"* theme.

During the event, a local philanthropic group called the "Angels Camp Boosters Club" held a frog jumping contest in commemoration of Mark's story. And *Vuala!* An eighty seven year old tradition was born.

Mark Twain left an indelible *"mark"* all over Angels Camp. As a kid, I went to *"Mark Twain Elementary School"*. . . We lived in a subdivision called *"Mark Twain Oaks"*. . . My mom worked at a Bank in the *"Mark Twain Shopping Center!"* And in High School, our mascot was a *"Bull Frog"*!

Anyway, that's my Town! Unique???

The Frog Jumping Stage At *'Frog Town'*

Statue of Mark Twain in Utica Park, Angels Camp

1986

WORLD RECORD
"ROSIE THE RIBITER"
21' 5 3/4"

LEE GIUDICI
SANTA CLARA, CA

ANGELS CAMP.
HOME OF THE JUMPING FROG.
ROMANCE - GOLD - HISTORY
FOUNDED IN 1849 BY GEORGE ANGEL, WHO ESTABLISHED
A MINING CAMP AND TRADING STORE 200 FEET BELOW
THIS MARKER. A RICH GRAVEL MINING AREA AND ONE
OF THE RICHEST QUARTZ MINING SECTIONS OF THE
MOTHER LODE. PRODUCTION RECORDS OF OVER 100
MILLION DOLLARS FOR ANGELS CAMP AND VICINITY.
PROMINENT IN EARLY DAY CALIFORNIA HISTORY.
TOWNSITE ESTABLISHED IN 1873. THE LOCALE OF
MARK TWAIN'S FAMOUS STORY, THE JUMPING FROG
OF CALAVERAS. FREQUENTED BY JOAQUIN MURIETTA,
BLACK BART AND OTHER EARLY DAY BANDITS.
ERECTED AND DEDICATED BY CALAVERAS COUNTY
CHAMBER OF COMMERCE. MAY 16, 1931.

"Ole" Twain n me talking about our books...
This lifesize bronze of Sam Clemens, sitting on a park
bench, graces the entrance of "Camps" restaurant
at the Greenhorn Creek golf course in Angels Camp.

O.K., the halftime commercial is over. . .
So let's get back to *Discovering!*

Volume 2

"The Journey Continues"

Coming up. . . In the Second Half of *"God's Gold!.."* We're going to discover more amazing patterns on the *"Daniel Vein."* But first, we're going to *re-visit* the *"Swastika Vein"*, I'll tell a few more cool stories, and we'll learn how the *"World of Numbers"* plays into the whole scheme of Millennialism.

PART 11

THE

CHASE

CONTINUES

The Swastika Vein Re-Visited
Twenty Years Later..

Dave from Brooklyn must have told me the story of the "Swastika Vein" two thousand times over the first two years of our partnership. In book one already covered the exciting part about the 25 ounces of gold that Dave and Chris discovered there, but I didn't tell you the rest of the story. . .

You see, after finding the big pocket, Dave, Chris, and Guy followed the vein deeper into the hillside. The vein widened from about an inch to nearly 'one foot' across. The *"Swastika Vein"* still had traces of gold in it, but it was hard for the guys to haul out wide rock samples. You see, the percentage of gold wasn't *that great* compared to the amount of rock that they had to haul out.

Meanwhile, both Chris and Guy got sick and passed away during the same year. They had been life-long friends, and in terms of gold mining, they were legends in Angels Camp. So Dave was left alone at the hillside mine. He began searching around for another spot to dig, and when winter hit, a landside caved-in the thirteen foot trench and covered up the Swastika vein! Besides that, a huge six ton rock rolled into on top of the rubble filled trench, and over the years that went by, poison oak grew in around the boulder.

Twenty years later, there it sat… And Dave always wished he could've followed that vein again. . . But with a degenerative hip problem, Dave had to 'hang up' his pick and shovel. He had dug there for twenty years, but he hasn't been back to the hillside mine for a least seven or eight. In our partnership, generally, I collected the samples, then brought them to his place and he did the washing.

I had seen the six ton boulder lots of times while searching for gold at the hillside mine, so I knew the exact location of the Swastika vein (right beneath that six ton boulder!). But the boulder was sunk down (like into a hole), so you couldn't just roll it out of the way. To make matters worse, the area was totally overgrown with poison oak! Dave would sometimes say *"forget it!, it's impossible. . ."* Then he would turn around and suggest a way to get around it, or dig beside the boulder. . . We considered using dynamite, but that was beyond our grasp.

Finally, one day I decided to start digging a hole next to the boulder. I knew the general area to shoot for to find the vein, and I wasn't going to stop digging until I found the *"wide part"* that Dave had told me about.

I also had to accept the fact, that, in order to recover the lead on the *"Swastika Vein,"* I was *just going to have to endure* catching a severe case of poison oak in the process. . . Which I did!

;:^O--ouch!

Friend "X" Shows Up

No sooner had I officially begun my quest to uncover the *Swastika Vein,* that one of my friends showed up on the scene. He wanted to help me on the quest. . .

He had been curious about my recent hard rock mining activities with Dave and asked if he could *"come out there with me,"* so that he could *see for himself how mining works.* Being a long-time friend, I cautiously let him in on our secret spot (on the agreement that he tell no one about the place!)

His family has lived in the County (and later in Angels Camp) since the gold rush days. We'll call him: Friend *"X"* because (for the purposes of this book) he wanted to remain sort-of anonymous. . Perhaps it was because I told him that I was going to brag about his father. . . You see, his dad was a hero in World War II. I heard a report from another friend, that his father was the *"spear-head"* for the liberation of the France at the boarder of northern Italy! Charles de Gaulle presented him the highest medal of honor in France, the *"Croix de guerre"*. I heard the story from my friend, Wayne, who saw the actual DD214 or "WD AGO" discharge papers that belonged to Friend *"X"s* dad, which told about his heroism and the award. He actually should have been awarded the congressional medal of honor in the U.S., but apparently, he never applied for it. I'm pretty sure he could be considered a National Hero.

Anyway, in the story that I heard, the Allies had taken the *"Boot of Italy"* and deposed the Fascist Dictator *"Benito Mussolini"* who moved into the northern part of Italy under the protection of Hitler and the Nazi's. Mussolini was the Axis friend and philosophical kin to Adolf Hitler and the Nazis. The Nazi's were firmly *'dug-in'* at the north between the boarders of France and Italy, and the Allies could not penetrate their defensive shield.

Meanwhile, Friend *"X"s* dad, being a very short, lean, and muscular guy (who ironically happened to be of French descent), bravely risked his life by crawling under the barb-wire laden trenches at night (across the enemy lines) and placed a pipe full of dynamite under the German machine gun platforms. Wham! It worked, and the Allies broke through and went on to liberate France from Nazi control.

Meanwhile, Back at the Mine. . .
A Plan Is Made. . .

As it turned out, Friend *"X"* was on vacation, and he had some time to kill. He offered to help out with my quest to recover access to the *"Swastika Vein."* He was really motivated. He suggested that we use cables and winches, and 20 ton house jacks, to lift and roll the boulder out of the way.

My plan was to dig a deep 'V' trench in front of the boulder so we could just roll it straight out of the depression using the cable winches. After a few days of intense work, *"X"* and we slowly lifted the boulder with the house jacks and winched the rock up and out. It rolled through the 'V' trench and down the hillside like a runaway train! The next two to three weeks were spent mucking out thirteen feet of dirt, rock, and poison oak roots. . . One bucket at a time. Meanwhile, friend *"X"* had to go back to his job, but he came out to visit and help on some of his days off.

Disappointment Follows. . .
The Swastika, But No Gold.

Finally, after a month from when my quest began, I reached the bottom, and actually found the spot where the vein turned like a Swastika, From there it turned into the direction of the hillside (just as Dave had said!). After more excavation I found the one foot wide section of the vein. . . But there was nothing. No gold. Maybe a couple of speckkks! What a bummer!

I left the Swastika Vein in defeat, and began digging around up by my old tunnel (the one that I had put on the back burner).

It was depressing, after doing all of that work, and catching a severe case of poison oak, just to find nothing. Friend "X" took it pretty well though. Apparently, he had enjoyed the experience. After his vacation, he continued to hang out with me at the hillside mine intermittently. But for me, the search for gold was not just a hobby, it was part of the way I supported my family, so I had a pretty strong drive to *"get the gold"*. . . And besides that, I had good reason to believe that Jesus wanted me to keep digging for gold, and to settle for no less than success. You see, it all started when I was a teenager. . .

"Seek My Wisdom Rather Than Gold"

A 30 Year Vacation From Hunting Gold

I first began prospecting for gold when I was in high school in the late seventies. My favorite spot to pan for gold was at Six Mile Creek on Lavi's property. When I was in the fifth grade my Dad bought seven acres of land from a guy that everyone called; *"Lavi"* (which was the shortened version of his Italian last name).

When we were growing up, we called our seven acre parcel of land *"the property"*. It was right next to Lavi's house and acreage. Lots of times our whole family (Mom, Dad, four kids, dog, and an occasional friend) would go visit Lavi in the evenings. *Lavi* had been a miner pretty much all of his life. I remember different times, seeing *Lavi* come out of a tunnel with an ore cart full of rock after blasting with dynamite. I sometimes watched him do blacksmith work on his picks and mining drills.

I remember one day being warned by my parents to stay in the front part of his house because he was burning off mercury down in the back! We used to spend a *LOT* of time out at *"the property."* In 1979 the price of gold reached an all-time high, and it seemed like *everyone* around Angels Camp was looking for gold back then. During that same time my

The Powder House at Lavi's
This is where the dynamite was stored!

grandfather (who was then ninety years old) began digging a 10-12 foot deep hole in his back yard and found gold at the bottom! He had worked in mines 'back in the day' and did mining of his own as well. He knew quite a bit about prospecting.

So there I was, looking for gold at the creek on Lavi's property. He told me how to look for gold in the cracks of the bedrock. I didn't know it at the time, but I was actually mining on the same site where the infamous "Joaquin Murrieta" had *his* claim back in the gold rush times. One day, I found a nugget that looked like half a brain. It was beautiful, but it looked like half of a brain! It was the biggest nugget I would find in thirty years. I was really *getting into* this gold mining thing, and I was trying to figure out how I could make it my full time gig.

Now I was also *"getting into Jesus"* during that time as well, and my favorite book in the Bible was Proverbs. Years later I began to commit the *Proverbs of Solomon* to memory.[66] Within a twelve chapter section (chapters: 10-22), there are close to 375 consecutive *'two liner'* proverbs (that's just about *one* proverb for every day of the year). And they hold application to probably *every* possible scenario of life. This invaluable arsenal of wisdom, from the renowned King Solomon, was meant to be memorized by young men, and made ready on the tongue.[66]

Now, it wasn't too long after I found the *"half brain nugget"* that the Lord began to speak to me about my life. While I was out on Lavi's creek panning gold, He seemed to keep saying to me over, and over, like from the book of Proverbs: *"Seek my wisdom rather than gold". . . "Seek my wisdom rather than gold". . .*

I don't know if he spoke one time, or a whole bunch of times, but I got the clear impression that Jesus didn't want me to go that direction anymore. . . So I just sort of *"hung it up"* and never let myself get *"gold fever".* . .

"The Silent Years"
Seeking His Wisdom

Shortly after that time, the price of gold started falling, I got busy with other things, and I just kind-a forgot about the gold. I've spent much of the last twenty five to thirty years doing work as an artist. Most of my work was in the area of interior design. The only *mining* I was involved in was mining for God's Wisdom. . .

Mining can be excruciatingly painful, and a lot of hard work. It can also be super discouraging, and frustrating (not to mention, *dangerous*.) But so far, the rewards have been worth it. Likewise, the pursuit of wisdom. . . Seeking God's Wisdom is just like mining. It's a patient search, with bouts of hard work. Whether it was seeking the Lord for wisdom in the field of art, or spending lots, and lots of lonely hours picking away at the revelations discovered on my *"Daniel Vein,"*. . .

Hey wait a minute!!! If I left the gold prospecting behind in the early 1980's, then why have I been telling of all these stories (from recent years) about hard rock mining and chasing pockets of gold in Mother Lode quartz veins? Well, that's the *other* part of my story. . . You see, about twenty five years after I *"gave up the gold"* I suddenly got the *"go ahead"* (from the

Lord) to start looking for gold again. . . Here's how it went down. . .

The Dream
Jesus The Prospector

Around the first day of Spring 2005 I had a dream. In the dream, a friend of mine was panning for gold in a wash tub, in the back of his shop, in downtown Angels Camp. As I was watched him swirl the gold pan under the water, I noticed that he had painted a *"mural"* in it! Painted on the gold pan, was a picture of a miner and a mule walking, with the sunrise behind them. They were walking towards the west. I got the impression that he had painted the pan *'just for the fun of it,'* but that it was also a business idea, a saleable product. It was odd that he would use the painted pan to look for gold as well.

In one of the scenes I recognized who my friend was. . . It was Jesus. . . And he was dressed like a Prospector! Interesting, I thought. . . The Lord has clearly given me a business/art idea. *This* was a door to a new level of art. Up until that time, I did a lot of "custom art" (where you work jointly with the customer on a project) Now, with these *"gold pans,"* I could have a chance to do more *"original art"*. I'm in the Gold Country. . . What a great idea. . . Unique, and low cost. . . The gold pan was both the canvas *and* the frame! I took out a business license with the name: *"Gold Rush Originals"* (original oil paintings on gold pans) and began painting them and hanging them around town.

Three and a half years later, because of the economic meltdown (2008), I quit getting calls for interior design work. I used to work with interior decorators *'on call'* out of my home for years, but when the housing market crashed things got a little dicey! So I thought it would be a good idea to open an art studio downtown Angels. That way (I figured), if I'm right on Main Street, I won't be "out of site and out of mind". So, I rented a little shop in downtown Angels Camp. And about a week or so later (while renovating the inside of the building) I realized something incredible. . . To my surprise, the shop I had rented, was the same place that was in my dream! It was on the same side of the street, it had the same front doorway. . . Apparently there was *more* to that dream than I had thought. I put in a wash-tub at the back of the shop so that people could pan for gold. The shop became just like my dream!

This image is taken from the gold pan that
I painted shortly after having the 'Jesus Dream'.
This was the basic scene I saw in Jesus' gold pan.
I use it for my shop logo at: "Gold Rush Originals".

Right at that same time, the price of gold
began to go *"through the roof"*! Also, a new T.V.
show came out about *hunting for gold in Alaska*,
and vacationers began calling me up on the
phone to see if I would take them out to my
"claim" to pan for gold! There is a longer version
to this story, but let's just say that I got the clear

message that Jesus was telling me that we were back in business looking for gold!

Now, it was around that same time that Dave from Brooklyn told me the location of his secret mining spot, and the rest of course is history. . .

Back To The Swastika Vein
Revived Hopes

Nearly a month had gone by since I had given up on the Swastika vein, but I decided to give it one more try. There was actually one more spot on the vein (between the wide and narrow section) that I had never really uncovered. I kept avoiding that area because it would have taken a whole days work to clear it out. Besides that, I think that there may have been a poison oak problem there as well. . . But I said *"what the heck"!* and started digging. For hours, I moved rock and debris until I uncovered the very last part of the vein. I took some samples home and… "Lo and behold," I found some pretty good gold! As days went by I even started finding some nice gold specimens in quartz! The Swastika vein was still producing!

Friend *"X"* continued to join me from time to time as I chased the vein and carved out a tunnel ten feet down and ten feet in horizontally. I kept going on it until I got into some really hard rock and the vein began to swirl around and pinch out here and there. Right at that point, I found a pocket! There was a lot of *color*, and specimens too, but one particular specimen felt pretty heavy! The quartz specimen had little specks of gold all over it, and when we hooked up an *electrical continuity tester* between the specks, we found that they were *all* connected to each other inside the rock. I wanted to know more, so I took the rock to my friend *"Ron, the Scientist"*. .

Ron The Scientist
In the Tradition of Archimedes

A man named Archimedes (287 B.C.-212 B.C.) lived during the first half of the Greek Empire (You can use the chart of the "Seven Empires" to map out this timeline). Archimedes was perhaps the most famous wise man (Scientist) of his day. The King had a crown made (so the story goes) by a goldsmith who later became suspect of replacing some of the gold with silver. The challenge was put forth by the King to Archimedes to find out the purity of the gold in the crown without messing up its form. Normally, they would simply melt the metal into a known measurable size, and then compare it to the known volume of pure gold.

No doubt the reward would be handsome, but Archimedes' reputation was on the line (he was supposed to be the "wise" man)! He simply *had* to find the answer to the King's dilemma! After a long while, Archimedes was still stumped, so he decided to relax, take a bath, and turn in for the night. His brain was so fried from trying to figure out the problem all day, that he forgot to turn off the water going into his bathtub. It had nearly overflowed, but he caught it just in time! Nevertheless, when Archimedes stepped into the bath, the water ran out over the rim of the tub and all over the floor! But instead of becoming upset at the spill, he ran out into the street naked Crying out; "Eureka!, Eureka!" (I've found it!, I've found it!) He was so excited about his discovery that he forgot to put on his clothes (so the story goes)! Archimedes was a Discoverer! He discovered that water will displace itself when an object is introduced into the same container. And that same principle is still being used today to find out the quantity of gold hidden in a quartz rock.

Ron "The Scientist" (as we like to call him) has been a good friend of mine for years now. I first got to know him and his wife through my interior design business (I did some artwork in their home in Angels Camp). But when I got into mining, I found out Ron was a miner as well. He owned a mine in Arizona and spent a few seasons there processing ore with cyanide.

Ron is a retired research scientist. And understandably, he likes to approach mining from a scientific standpoint. I've learned a lot about the chemical aspects of recovering gold from Ron. I don't see him as much as I used to, since he moved back to Arizona after his wife passed away. A very pleasant individual, possessing a strong sense of skepticism and logical reasoning, Ron was the guy with the tools of knowledge that came in handy for the pursuit of gold. And when I had gold to sell, he was also one of my "buyers."

When I showed Ron the rock with gold specks all over it, he went right to work on the project. He found a formula for figuring out the content of gold trapped in quartz. First we weighed the rock dry. Then, we weighed the rock submerged in water. We then multiplied the dry weight by something like 1.9, and multiplied the submerged weight by another number, like 3.1. After that, we subtracted the difference and calculated the quantity of gold that should be in the rock. We guessed it to be 10 grams. That's about a 1/3rd of a Troy ounce!

After the *"guessing game"* was over, Ron wanted to verify our prediction. So he got ahold of some hydrofluoric acid which dissolves silica (the main component of quartz), but leaves the gold untouched! And over the next two weeks we dissolved away the rock until there was nothing left but gold! There was a big swirly piece of gold left behind. And some little loose pieces and dust as well. After weighing it all up, it came to exactly 10 grams! The formula worked great, Ron was thoroughly satisfied with the experiment, and Dave, friend "X", and I had some cash in our pockets. . .

One more thing about Ron (which will add to the irony of the Swastika Vein story). Ron's brother was in Italy around the same time that Friend "X"s dad was there. After Friend "X"s dad helped the Allies break through the Northern Italian blockade, Mussolini and his Mistress, Clara Petacci, tried to escape into Switzerland, but were apprehended. They were summarily executed and hung upside-down on meat hooks from the rafters of an Esso gas station in Milan. Meanwhile, Ron's brother, an MP (Military Police), was sent with a contingency of MP's to recover the bodies. Ron's brother helped take down the bodies from the makeshift gallows!

There you have it! Out of the Swastika vein, discovered by Dave "the Jew" from Brooklyn, came the biggest pocket of gold in his life. And after re-opening the Swastika Vein, with the help of Friend "X" (the son of the famous Fascist and Nazi fighter), and I chased the vein until I discovered my biggest chunk of gold yet. I then sold it to Ron, the Brother of the guy who literally *'had a hand'* in taking down the symbol of fascism (the common kin of Nazism)!

The gold that I found on the Swastika Vein was nowhere near the amount found by Dave and Chris, but it turned out to be the largest amount of gold I have ever found in one rock to date.

Top left: The Quartz is being dissolved in Hydroflouric Acid leaving gold behind.

Middle: Nearly a 10 Gram chunk of gold! Left behind after the quartz was dissolved.

Top Rright: Other loose gold left behind from the dissolved quartz specimen.

PART 12

THE
SCIENCE
OF
NUMBERS

FAST-TRACK, BY-PASS TO DISCOVERY > > >
Continue Here: Read to Page 206:

Ancient Wisdom
The World Of Numbers

The Bible is filled with spiritual and religious truths associated with numbers (I mean hey, there's even a book in the Old Testament of the Bible called; *"The Book of Numbers"!*). But seriously, the *world* of numbers can be both a place of profound mystery as well as a place of profound clarity of ideas. Numbers convey thoughts and communicate ideas. No doubt, every ancient civilization and religion has incorporated numbers, geometry, or some other form of mathematical language as a basis for explaining mysteries about their belief systems. What we refer to today as; *'Mathematics'* and *'Geometry'*, the ancients would have referred to as; *'Wisdom'* or *'Knowledge*[36].

An Ancient Babylonian Cuneaform Shard Showing Numbers Would Look Like This...

The Latin word for; *'Knowledge'* is *"scientia"* from which we get "science". So I suppose a "Scientist" is literally *a 'Knowledg-ist'!* Now the word; *'mathematics'* is derived from the Greek word *"mathemata"*, which translates out to;

"science of learning". That's why Mathematicians are always learning. . . It's endless knowledge.

Anyway, you get the point, *"Science"*. . . *"Math"*. . . It's all about *Wisdom* and *Knowledge*, patterns and measuring!

Aside from basic practical considerations (like trade and commerce), the ancient wisdom[36] was used for astronomical or astrological calculations, the magical arts,[37] and the building of the pyramids. It seems that *some* people have dedicated their lives to the study of the *'measurements'* connected to the *Great Pyramid of Giza.*

Hey, by the way!. . . Speaking of the pyramids. . . Take a look at the picture from the front cover of "God's Gold" (below). . .

This awesome specimen is actually a naturally formed crystal of gold in the form of a pyramid. It is <u>by far</u> the best specimen of gold that I have ever discovered (to date). I found it when we were tearing into a 4" wide quartz vein at an old mine site behind my friend's house (a half hour drive from my home in Angels Camp!)

Friend *"X"* was there with me. Before I discovered and picked up the rock with the gold pyramid in it, *"X"* had found a different specimen with a metal detector. As it turned out, the piece that *"X"* found was the matching piece of quartz that broke away from the pyramid specimen. It contained a hidden piece of gold that looked like a cobra snake!

Above: The matching piece of Quartz that broke away from the pyramid crystal.

And here's something weird. . . If the rock hadn't broken open, the complete specimen would have looked like a cobra snake balancing on the point of the pyramid! (see illustration below)

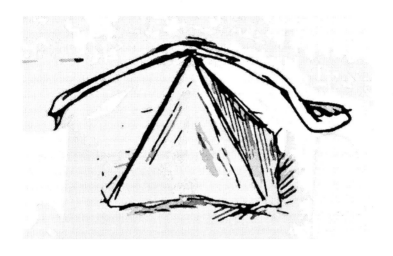

We sold the specimen to a collector from Germany for a handsome bundle of cash. But we're confident that we will find more rare specimens where *that* one came from. They say that when you find one unusual gold formation (like the pyramid), then there will generally always be *more* of the same throughout the rest of the vein! Who knows, we could very possibly break into a million dollar pocket on that vein!

The Amazing Number Seven
The Holy Number

Some people hear the term; *'numerology'* and immediately equate the term with occultism, wizardry, fortune tellers, and the like (of which the Bible warns are unclean and spiritually dangerous things.[36]) But there is a *"holy"* and *"clean"* kind of numerology, and we find it conveyed throughout the entire Bible.[37]

The Book of Proverbs speaks about the Seven Pillars of Wisdom. The book of Revelation speaks about the *"Seven Spirits of God"*. And in the book of Genesis of course, we hear of the first *"Seven days"* of the Creation. Peter asked the Lord if he should forgive someone only up to *"seven"* times. . . Jesus replied by telling Peter he had better upgrade it to *"Seventy times Seven"* That's 490 times!

Both the Bible <u>and</u> Millennialism are "all about" the number seven! No doubt, you've heard terms such as; *"lucky number seven"*, and *"seven eleven"*. I don't know about the 'lucky part', but there are mathematical and geometrical factors associated with the number seven which are quite fascinating. The reason they say: *"seven eleven"* is because there is a geometrical relationship between those two numbers. Here's what I mean. . .

The *'foundation'* of a circle is its *diameter*. When we make the diameter *seven*, and draw a half circle from the two ends of the diameter, the circumference *'arc'* comes *really close* to eleven!

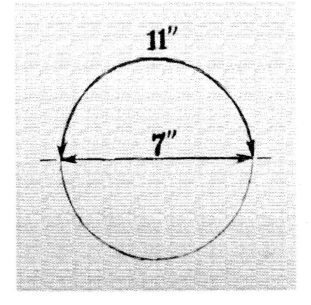

Millennium of course is all about the number *seven*. Let's look at some examples of the unique role that the number seven plays in our world. . . We'll begin on the next page. . .

"In Music"

There are Seven Major notes in the musical scale (These notes are the 'white' keys on the piano). Every 'eighth' note is actually the first note in a repeating pattern that begins a new set of seven notes. It seems like there are a b'jillion notes, but there are really only seven major notes.

' Light and Rainbows'

There are seven colors in the rainbow: Red, Orange, Yellow, Green, Blue, Indigo, and Violet!

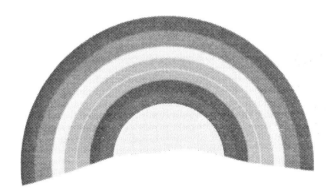

"The Chemical Elements"

The periodic table of elements is sort of complicated. . . If you've ever taken a science or chemistry class, then you know what it looks like. When you look at the chart, you can see that there are seven horizontal rows with some of the spaces missing here and there.

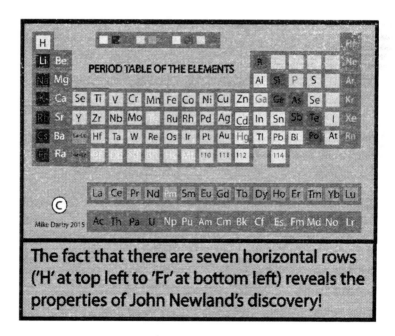

The fact that there are seven horizontal rows ('H' at top left to 'Fr' at bottom left) reveals the properties of John Newland's discovery!

Another set of two horizontal rows below the seven. These two actually represent parts of the bottom two of the seven (row 'six' and row 'seven'). It was arranged this way so the chart could be condensed. Looks kind-a confusing doesn't it! But the fact that there are seven horizontal rows (H at top left) to (Fe at bottom left)

The present day chart came about after the prodigious pioneering work of men such as the nineteenth century Englishman John Newlands, and Dimitri Mendeleev (Mendeleev was from Russia). Mendeleev gets much of the credit for the development of the chart of elementals, but Newlands made a discovery showing that behavioral traits among the elements follow a pattern of octaves. Just like the pattern of seven in the musical scale!

When Newlands proposed his findings to the Chemistry Society in 1866, he was met with ridicule. They didn't want to publish his discovery, because they thought it may be *"controversial"*. Controversial? . . . Later, the Society finally credited Newlands for his amazing discovery (with a gold medal) five years after they recognized Mendeleev's work. In 2008 the Royal Chemistry Society installed a historical plaque upon the house where John Newlands was born in honor of his unique work as the discoverer of the periodic law of the chemical elements!

What was up with those guys from the *Chemistry Society?* Apparently, many in the scientific community "can't seem to see the forest for the trees." Or perhaps they don't really *want* to see the forest, because it crosses over into the Mystical, or Spiritual and Religious realm of knowledge. An amazing interrelated order and harmony exists within the universe which it is not necessarily that mysterious or complicated to understand. . . It's the mystical harmony of the number 'Seven.'

This mindset (like the apparent mindset of some of those in the Chemistry Society) seems especially entrenched when the harmony and order appears to be tied to longstanding Biblical revelation, or religious wisdom that preceded the *"age enlightenment"* (to which modern science evidently owes their allegiance.) Step back and have a look, and you will find that everything in creation seems to be crying out 'Seven'!

' Gestation cycles'

Now don't quote me on this one, but this next *'snippet'* sounded pretty intriguing, so I added it in to the collection about 'Seven.' Apparently *some* have suggested that many of the gestation periods of animals are based upon the number seven.

Supposedly, the developmental time from conception to birth in most creatures of the animal kingdom is determined by multiples of days times seven! i.e. Horses: 343 days (49 x7 days), rats: 21 days (3 x7 days), and human beings like you and me. . . 280 days (40x7 days).

'Gambling'

(statistical science)

Here's one for the gamblers out there... A dice cube has six *'faces'*. Each face is marked with dots signifying a different number (1 thru 6). When tossing a pair of dice, the chances of landing a 'snake eyes' (1 and 1) are only one time in every thirty six rolls of the dice.

The chances of throwing a combination of *'three'* are twice as likely than a *'two'* (That's one time in eighteen rolls of the dice). But a 'seven' on the other hand, comes up more often than any other combination! It comes up one time for every six rolls of the dice. . . Notice the role that the numbers six and seven hold in this six sided geometric form of entertainment that we call throwing dice? The dice have six faces. . . a 'seven' lands every *six* throws. . . Hey, what are the chances?

'Geometry'

Start with a symmetrically perfect cube. Now, let's begin aligning cubes (of the same exact size and proportion) next to each other in their shortest sequence, until another perfect cube is formed (see the chart below). From the initial cube, it takes exactly seven steps to re-create the form of a cube again! This process is similar to the way of the octave on the musical scale. The 'octave cube' comes back to the exact same form as the first. The volume changes, yet the form never changes, but simply repeats within a framework directly related to the number seven!

[I've included a few more examples of some of the unique properties of the number seven in a section in the back of the book entitled: "God's Gold! Extras". (see pages 317-320.) 'Check it out!']

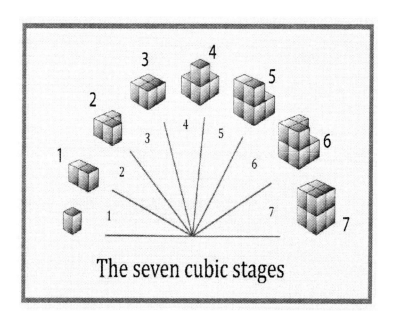

The seven cubic stages

'The Meaning of Seven'

From a religious or spiritual standpoint, many will tell you that the number seven symbolizes spiritual perfection or completion. This is absolutely so, but do they know why? Actually, the numerological meaning behind the number seven is laid out quite plainly in the very first book of the Bible. Most people may not even realize it, but from the very first page, the Bible begins laying down a framework consisting of the number seven. Here's what I mean. . . The very first pages of the very first book of the Bible (Genesis) begins with a story about the first *"seven"* days of the created universe. Moses (whom the book of Genesis is attributed) say's that God accomplished all the work of creation in seven days (actually the work was done in six days, then he took a *'day off'* to rest).[40]

Those *seven* days made up the very first week, and that first week is called; *'the Foundation of the World'.* We may also call it; *'the foundation of the time'.* The creation of the Heavens and Earth can be likened to a great big *'construction project'* which took only *six* days to complete. Pretty amazing if we compare the Lord's time schedule to that of any modern day construction outfit!

In the perfection of God's Wisdom and Power, He unleashed his awesome strength and creative design capabilities for six consecutive days, thus creating the heavens, the earth, and all that is within them. That's a lot of power and wisdom! Apparently, after six days he was exhausted, so he rested for one day.

In all of this we can see that the number seven reflects the perfection and completion of God's power and his wisdom. But there is a pattern within the number seven as well. . . Namely, a pattern consisting of 'the six' and then 'the seventh'. . .

Jewish Geometry
"A Star Is Born"

Now we're going to shift the gears a little bit... I'm beginning to lead you into a realm of understanding which shows that the number *'seven'* possesses a unique relationship with the number *'six'* as well.

Let's start out by doing a little *"hands on"* experiment. . . Take a penny and place it on the table or desk. . . Now start placing other pennies around it. . . How many pennies will fit around the first penny?

THE ANSWER IS ON THE NEXT PAGE. . . . .

Exactly six pennies fit around the first one! The pennies make a beautiful pattern. We see this pattern in the honey comb, we see it in snowflakes.

We can also see this pattern emblazoned on the flag that represents the modern day Nation of Israel. The pattern on Israel's flag is known as; the 'Star of David'[41]. . .

The "Star Of David"

I love Geometry! The configuration of seven pennies creates a primary geometric model displaying the number 'seven' in a way that is quite different than simply a row of seven digits. It shows us that there is actually more to the number seven than simply seven digits, or seven '1,1,1,1,1,1,1's'. There is something 'nice' about it, something beautiful. There is something else going on here. . . Do you get the drift?

A unique Relationship between Six and Seven

At first glance, the honeycomb, the snowflakes, and the "Star of David" have the appearance of six, but as you can see (in light of the configuration of the pennies) they actually *'take in'* the number seven as well.

In the *Star of David* there are seven pennies in all, yet there is an inseparable relationship with the number six as well.

According to tradition, King David inscribed

this geometric design upon his 'shield of battle', and it has now become an inseparable part of Jewish identity. The origin of the *star* is up to debate,[41] but if David *did* use the symbol, what did it mean?

Well. . . actually, the Star of David is a geometric picture that represents the "foundation of time" as it was handed down to us by Moses! Namely, the six days of creation revolving around the one unique day (the seventh day in which God rested)! Therefore, if you think about it, the Star of David (being displayed on the national flag of Israel) could be considered a confession of faith to the whole world, proclaiming that God made the heavens and the earth in six days and rested on the seventh. Can you see how this geometric pattern corroborates Moses's story about *"the beginning"* of all things? Is this stuff deep and profound or what?

Therefore, the geometric configuration of the pennies sheds light into the mystery of why God created the universe over a of seven day period of time, as opposed to say, for example, eight days, or four days, or even 5 billion years...etc.). Here's how: The pennies (with their perfect and consistent geometrical forms) cannot be configured in a *'tighter'* form other than the *'six around the one'* pattern. I believe that these things (like geometric form) reflect or portray something about the eternal attributes of God himself (just as stated by the Apostle Paul.

From a geometrical standpoint, it just makes sense that the nature of the Creator, and the work that he did creating everything, *couldn't* have happened any other way!

Subsequently, when we consider the 'bigger picture' of the seven thousand year Millennial Cycle (which is derived from the foundational *'week'* of creation) the *'penny configuration'* (*"Star of David"*) is a geometrical witness of the truth (or at least to the 'logic' behind the creation story written in Genesis), and is therefore a *"witness"* to the Millennial teaching as well.

FAST-TRACK, BY-PASS TO DISCOVERY > > >
Skip Ahead. . .Go To Page 222:

PART 13

THE

RHYTHM

The Heartbeat of Creation
And The Millennial Cycle

When the *"foundation of the world"* was laid, a rhythm of time was established. A rhythm which is based upon the first seven days. I refer to this *rhythm* as; *"the heartbeat of God's creation"*.

Moses wrote down not only the account of the creation in Genesis (which is based on 'six' plus *'the seventh'*), but he also wrote down an entire code of laws which told the people how to live in harmony with both God, and with everyone (and everything else) in His Creation.[42]

Out of all the laws which Moses handed down to the Israelites, a number of them were stamped with the unique seal consisting of the pattern; 'six' plus 'the seventh' (the "heart beat of God's creation"). Let's take a quick look at a few of these laws:

'The Law of Weeks of Days'

The first law that reflected the 6 and 7th rhythm was the law concerning 'weeks of days'. In commemoration of the *'first week of creation,'* the Israelites were to work *six* days, then, on the seventh day, they were to celebrate a feast day. On the seventh day, everyone was given a chance to *'rest'* from all of their labor (the Sabbath day). This was the law of *'weeks of days'*.

'The Law of Weeks of Years'

After this, there were other laws that had to do with a *'week of years'*. In Israel, the contract between a master and his servant was to be no longer six years[43] and in the seventh year the servant was to be released from duty with severance pay. Also, in the orchards of Israel, the fruit trees were to be pruned six years in a row, but in the seventh year they were not to be cut back[44] The seventh year was a time for the tree branches to 'let it all hang out' (so to speak). The same rule applied for the plowing of the fields. . . There were six years of plowing and one year to let the ground lay fallow. The word;

'Septilee' is the word that has been used to describe this seven year period of time.

'The Law of the Jubilee Year'

Next, there was a law that had to do with a set of (seven) seven year periods. After 49 years there was a special year of Jubilee.[45]. . In the *'year of Jubilee'* a national land redistribution program went into effect. Everyone who had sold (leased) their properties were allowed to return to their ancestral inheritances. In the *'year of Jubilee'* all lands reverted back to the original family owners.

It could be asserted however (as it probably has been), that these laws were just arbitrary ideas put forth by a kooky old man named Moses who had an *'obsessive compulsive'* affinity for numerological order and the number seven. No... but rather, these laws were put in place by Moses because they reflect the basic pattern of the foundation of all created things (the *"heartbeat"* of God's creation).

During the French revolution a Humanist regime tried to get rid of the seven day week because it reminded them of God and the Christian Faith. In fact, they instituted an entirely new calendar based on the number 'ten'. For about ten years, a ten day week was implemented (there were nine work days, and the *'tenth'* day was a day of rest)[46] Needless to say, the *'base ten'* week was a complete failure.[47] People and animals alike began to get sick, and chaos ensued. But soon enough, everybody got back into the *'beat'* again, and the seven day week made a comeback. It's a good thing to keep in rhythm with the heartbeat of God's creation. . . Don't have a heart attack!

The Law Of God
After The Days Of Moses

A complete jubilee cycle lasted 50 years, but the rhythm didn't stop there... We can tell from the Biblical record that an even greater cycle exists. It is a cycle of *'ten'* jubilees (490-500 years). I like to call these 500 year cycles; "The Eras of the Bible. Moses never actually prescribed a law that dealt with any cycle of time longer than 50 years, but he <u>did</u> sort of predict a few major events about the Nation's future that ended up happening every 500 years! (i.e. the *choosing of a king*, the *Babylonian captivity*, and *the first coming of Christ*)![48]

500 years after the days of Moses, the people asked for a king, and 500 years after that, the people went into Captivity in Babylon. Again, 500 years after the Babylonian captivity, was the coming of Christ! The Bible reveals a total of *"nine"* 500 year eras. This pattern of 500 year eras can be traced back to the beginning in Genesis. Moses recorded the history of most of the first four eras by means of his personal prophetic revelation. Now the rest of the Old Testament records the sixth, seventh, and eighth eras. And of course the New Testament records the first part of the ninth Era.

See chart on next page. . .

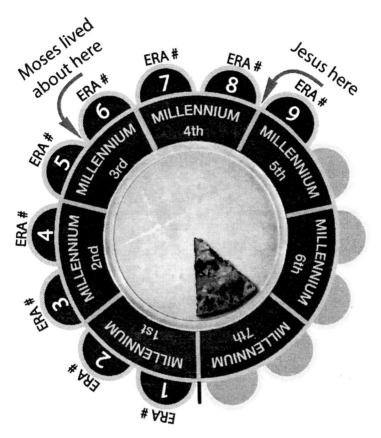

There were eight 'Biblical Eras'
from Adam till Christ...

More Evidence For The 500 Year Cycle
The House Of God

This same 500 year Era pattern is also connected to the dwelling places of God. In other words, every 500 years the Lord got a new house!

Here's what I mean. . .   When Moses fashioned the twelve tribes of Israel into a bona fide nation, and gave them the laws to live by, he also built a house for the God of Israel to dwell in. The house of the lord was actually a tent (and a very nice one to say the least!).

This *'Tent of God'* came complete with a company of servants (the Priests and Levites). Their job was to run the affairs of God's dwelling place.[49] In essence, the Priests and Levites were God's household servants. The Priests were a higher class of servant than the Levites, and the *'High Priest'* would be likened to the *'chief'* or *'head'* servant).

In the English tradition the *'Butler'* is the *'head servant'*, and is in charge of all the other servants in the household. He answers only to the owner of the house. Therefore we could say that the High Priest was the *Butler* of God's house!

Anyway, 500 years after Moses established this whole system, a total renovation of the Nation took place, and the *"kingdom years"* began in Israel. It was at the beginning of that era, King David and his son Solomon designed and built a *'proper house'* for the Lord in Jerusalem.[50] The new house was called the *'Temple'* (which simply means *'house'*). In the days of King David, a new family line was established for the High Priestly order, the family of Zadok.[51]

At the end of the *"Kingdom years"*, Solomon's Temple was burned to the ground by the King of Babylon, and the people were carried away to become slaves in the land of Babylon.[52] Seventy years later the Jews came back from their captivity and began to build a new Temple. At that time, Ezra became the high priest and led a major reformation, in terms of teaching the common people the laws and way of God.[53]

The second renovation and restructuring took place about 500 years from the beginning of the kingdom years and the building of Solomon's Temple, until a new Temple was re built after Solomon's was destroyed by the Babylonian's in 586 B.C.!

Then, 500 years after the post Babylonian restructuring (during the days of Jesus of Nazareth) we see that Herod the Great began doing a major renovation of the Jerusalem Temple.[54]

Solomon

Gustave Dore'

20/20 Hindsight

I f we carefully look back over the Biblical history, it's becomes obvious that things changed every 500 years. Every era, a total renovation and restructuring of the nation took place, and God got a new house! In the chart below, see how the daily cycles went from *'weeks'* of seven days, all the way up to a Biblical Era which lasts 500 years?

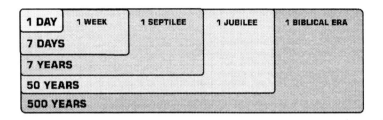

But now, let's take this up a notch…. Two '500' year eras make up a Millennium. There's actually a *'thousand year pattern'* in the Biblical record as well (these are the patterns I was referring to on page 59., which first motivated my quest to study at Hawaii.) If we count one thousand years from the beginning, we come to the days of Enoch who lived in the Anti-Diluvian (pre-flood) world.[58] Enoch was the most famous man of God in his day. . .

And from the days of Enoch until the days of Abraham (the father of the nation of Israel) there were one thousand years. . . And from the days of *Abraham* until the greatest days of Israel's history (the establishment of the Kingdom of Israel through King David) you guessed it. . . 'one thousand years'! And from *King David* to *Jesus of Nazareth*, 'one thousand years'! Now the cycles didn't stop there. . . If we kept following the pattern, we would probably find that these cycles have continued on right through, until the present day! There is definitely something going on here!

Through all of these things when we look at the *"BIG PICTURE"* of history in light of the Biblical revelation of past, present, and future, we can see that there is a rhythm in the flow of world history based upon the first seven days of the creation of the Universe. . . It's a *'rhythm'* which has been *'keeping the beat'* throughout Biblical history, in a pattern that *'jives'* with the Millennial teaching.

Understand the logic?

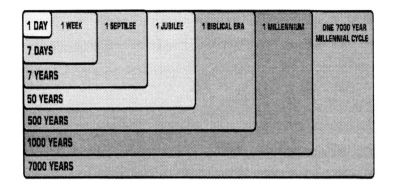

1 DAY	1 WEEK	1 SEPTILEE	1 JUBILEE	1 BIBLICAL ERA	1 MILLENNIUM	ONE 7000 YEAR MILLENNIAL CYCLE
7 DAYS						
7 YEARS						
50 YEARS						
500 YEARS						
1000 YEARS						
7000 YEARS						

Somebody said: *"the numbers don't lie"*. . .
Well, that statement is true (if all the numbers add up). And at this point you can probably see for yourself, that things seem to be *'adding up'* in terms of the numerological meaning behind the number *'seven'*, as well as patterns in the flow of Biblical and World history as they relate to the logic behind the concept of a 7000 year Millennial cycle. Pretty fascinating huh? It makes sense!

PART 14

MORE

PATTERNS

FAST-TRACK, BY-PASS TO DISCOVERY > > >
Continue Here: Read to Page 232:

The *Daniel* Vein Re-Visited
Another Pattern

Just like a persistent miner would do (and kind-of the way I re-opened the "Swastika vein"), I kept pursuing the "Daniel Vein" to see what else I could find it.   And as I re-evaluated the *Pattern of the Seven Empires*, I considered something else. If the 'rise and fall' of the Seven Empires fell on exact *"sevenths,"* then what would happen if I divided the pattern into *"thirds"?* Here's what I found. . .

The history of Western Civilization can be divided into three basic periods of time;

1. The *'Classical Period'*. . .

2. The *'Middle Ages'*. . .

3. The *'Modern Era'*. . .

1. The *Classical Period* were those times when most of the people wore *'Togas'*. . .

2. In the *Middle Ages* (also known as; the *Mediaeval Period*, or the *'Dark ages'*) people wore what looked like pajamas and hoods, like stocking caps. . .

3. In the *Modern Era* people began wearing *'super fancy'* clothing!

All joking aside, these are the three basic eras of *'Western Civilization'*. The *'official'* beginning of the *'Middle Ages'* are usually identified by historians as having started either with *"the reign of Constantine"*, or with the *"fall of Rome"* (not the *Empire*, but rather, the *City*, along with its entire social and political infrastructure, around the year 445 A.D.) The City of Rome was invaded three times over a period of seventy years (410-476 A.D.) by Barbarian hordes and the Huns (Attila).

As they looked at their crumbled world, the *Classical Roman Pagan's* blamed Christian's, and the laws put into place by Constantine (which favored the *new Christian God*, over the *old Roman gods*) for the destruction of the City, because the traditional gods of Rome had been forsaken and were no longer willing to protect the City.

In his literary masterpiece *"the City of God'*, the Christian Philosopher/Monk; *St. Augustine*, explained that the destruction of Rome was due to a buildup of *wickedness* and *debauchery* by the Roman people. Augustine was a Philosopher in the vein of the Greek tradition, in fact, he is considered to be one of the *Greatest Western Philosophers*.

Aristotle on the other hand, is considered to have been the *"Greatest of All"*. He is referred to in Academia simply as; *"The Philosopher"*, but Augustine spoke of Aristotle in a *dimmer* light, he referred to him as; *"that blind Pagan!"* Augustine's work received great reviews, and his teaching laid the foundation for a *whole new* cultural system in the west, a *"Christianized"* culture which lasted through the entire period of time which is now called; the *Middle Ages*.

The official *"end"* of the Middle Ages (and subsequent *beginning* of the Modern Era) took place due to something called; the *"Renaissance"* (which came about as a result of a resurgence of interest in the ancient works of the Greek Philosophers, mainly that of Aristotle (around the year 1223 A.D.).

The *'Middle Ages'* are sometimes referred to as; the *"dark ages"* because during that time the *'Light'* of the *Classical Philosophers* (like Aristotle) was dim at best, or totally absent in the minds of those in the West, and no doubt, probably due to the massive influence of Augustine. But the Post Medieval Renaissance generation practically *"Deified"* Aristotle (that's *deified*, not *defied*. In other words, they practically turned him into a god) Aristotle's logic and reason blew the minds of that generation.

The new fascination with the Greek philosophical works, and a renewed knowledge of the amazing technological wonders of the Classical Greco-Roman world (which was a product of the Greek philosophical movement) produced a new *'Humanism'* in the west. Many at that time feared that the Christian culture in the West would soon lapse altogether into a Philosophically Atheistic, or Pagan culture. In the year 1223 A.D. the *'man of the hour'* was Thomas Aquinas. It is said that Thomas *"saved"* Western Christianity from going Pagan. He single handedly *'took on'* Aristotle and his Logic, and came up with a synthesis between Christianity's *'Faith'* and Aristotle's *'Reason'*. Thomas' *synthesis* may not have been perfect, but it created a basis for many of the members of Western Civilization to be *'free thinkers'* while at

the same time, still able to *hold on* to certain *dogmatic* ideas of the Christian faith.

The Renaissance also brought about a *new kind* of focus on the *individual*, as opposed to the *community*. An emphasis on the *'Many'* versus the *'One.'* {I don't have the space here to really get into it, but just as there were the three great Greek Philosophers: Socrates, Plato, and Aristotle, (and each one had a unique way of perceiving the world) so also, It could be said that the three eras of Western Civilization separately reflect the mindsets of those three Great Philosophers of Greece (perhaps Augustine thought like Plato, and Thomas thought like Aristotle.)

It could easily go without saying, but huge technological and social advances were made as Western Europeans began to *'de-centralize'* during this 'third era' of Western Civilization. All of this officially began with the *Renaissance.* We call this period of time; the 'Modern Era'.

When the 2,333.333 year period is divided into thirds, the divisions fall precisely on the years; 445 A.D., and 1223 A.D.!

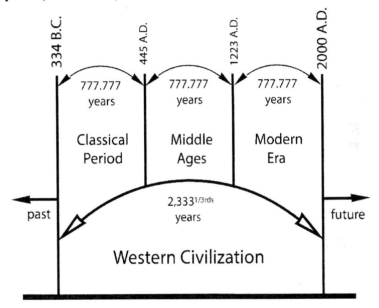

The Three Periods of Western Civilization

The Classical Period; 334 B.C. to 445 A.D., the Middle Ages; 445 A.D. to 1223 A.D., and the Modern Era; 1223 A.D. to 2000 A.D.

Isn't it *'weird'* that the *Middle Ages* were literally *'in the middle'* of Western history?

In the exact middle! ! !

Yet Another Pattern!
The Holy Roman Empire

One of the greatest figures in western history was Charlemagne. He was member of the Carolingian Empire, which was a royal family bloodline that spanned the entire 333.333 years of the empires existence. Even though Charlemagne was just one of the many other Carolingian Kings, he stood out like a giant. As a matter of fact, he was actually seven feet tall! Anyway, Charlemagne created an unusual new political entity in Europe. It became an overarching *'empire of empires'* with Franco/Italian and Germanic roots. Charlemagne died around the year 814 A.D. and shortly after his death they started calling it: *"Holy Roman Empire."* This new European political entity continued all the way into the twentieth century.

Much more could be said about the Holy Roman Empire, but just notice this one thing: when the 2,333.333 year period is divided in two parts, the halfway point falls precisely on the year 834 A.D. This is amazing!

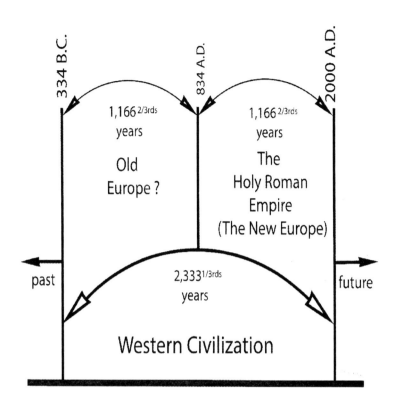

ALEXANDER'S
"One World Order"
Has His Dream Finally Come True?

These things are truly amazing! Something is definitely going on here! What does this recurring 333.333 year pattern mean. . . And what about the *'push'* towards democratization and world government?

Do you see how the expansion and influence of Western Civilization has literally covered the entire face of the Earth?

But what *"in the world"* will happen next? Will yet another empire rise from obscurity and be destined to rule for exactly 333.333 years, or has Alexander's dream of a *'One World Order'* finally come to fruition?

I don't believe another Empire is in the cards for Western Civilization. Rather, it looks to me like all seven empires, each one fulfilling their own predetermined lifespan of 333.333 years, have just now completed a great common purpose. . .

Like relay runners passing one another the Olympian torch, the seven empires together (all of them 'rising and falling' like clockwork) have finally actualized Alexander's dream of 'Total World Domination.' And over a collective period of lasting exactly $1/3^{rd}$ of 7000 years. . . And which also (by the way) was completed just at the *end* of the Sixth Millennium!

Let's pull up the Millennial Pizza Chart from page 144 and look at the big picture. . . (see chart illustration on the opposite page).

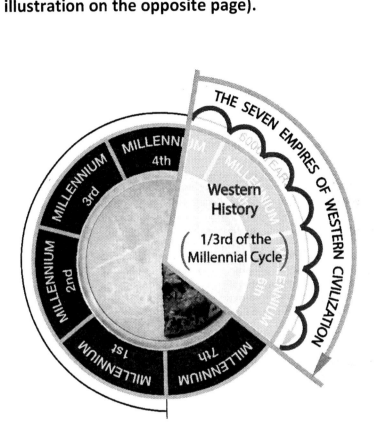

The Seven Empires, over a period of time lasting 1/3rd of 7000 years!

FAST-TRACK, BY-PASS TO DISCOVERY > > >
Skip Ahead. . .Go To Page 240:

Pure Gold
God's Gold. .

No doubt, all of these things have something to do with Alexander and his dream of a *'One World Order,'* but they also have something to do with the fulfillment of the *'Times of the Gentiles,'* the restoration of the *'Lost Kingdom of Israel,'* and the Second Coming of Israel's King: Jesus Christ!

The book of Proverbs say's wisdom is better than gold, and knowledge is more valuable than silver. The discovery of these patterns are a pure revelation of Wisdom and Knowledge from God's Word. . .

This is Gold. . . God's Gold. . .

Directly from the Daniel Vein!

THE

4TH

QUARTER

old on now! We're going into the fourth quarter. PART 16 is going to bring us into a *whole new perspective* of looking at the 2333.333 year period of time, as well as the meaning behind the stupendous success of Western Civilization.

This *New Perspective* will all begin when we hit the book of Revelation, and discover an intriguing connection about Angels. . .

When I consider the success and expansion of *Western Man's* influence, it looks to me like fodder for a conspiracy theory.
Wouldn't you say?. . .

Absolutely. Without a doubt. . . There *has* in fact been a conspiracy underway for *"total world domination"*, but it has not been a *conspiracy of Men*. . . But rather of *Angels!* No, not *Angels Camp!* I'm talking about *"Angels,"* like *"Michael"* the Archangel.

PART 16

THE

ANGELIC

CONNECTION

Angels
What's In A Name?

Many people, when they first hear the name of my home town (Angels Camp), assume that the town may have experienced (at one time or another, in its history) an unusual occurrence involving *angelic activity*.

Actually, the town is named after a guy named Henry Angel. Henry moved out from Rhode Island and discovered gold in the creek. Henry was the first to set up a tent and sell supplies to the rush of people flooding into the area to look for gold! Now there are conflicting stories about a brother named George Angel. The historians are still trying to get *that* story straightened out. But we have a picture of Ole Henry, and we know exactly where he set up his Camp beside the creek that runs through town!

"Angels From Hell!"
Un-Welcome Visitors

When I was a kid *EVERYBODY* used to come up to Angels Camp in May for the *'Frog Jump'* at the County Fair Grounds (the Frog Jump took place we just called it The *Frog Jump*). The Fair and Frog Jump was a lot of fun, but for me (not to mention plenty of other people) it was *kind-of-a* scar-r-r-y time of year as well. The reason being, you see, is that the Fair tended to bring in a few "un-welcome guests" to our nice little town. . . Namely, lawless motorcycle gangs like *"The Hell's Angels"*!

For a little guy like me living in the 1960's, the *"Hell's Angels"* were a hell-u-va sight to watch. Out of nowhere, around the Fair time, like a hoard of locusts, they would roll into town. And even though my friends and I were scared to death of these *'Bikers'*, we thought that their *"choppers"* (as well as some of their women) were cool! I also liked the smell of the Patchouli oil that wafted through the air. . .

But in 1972 my family *"headed out"* to Nevada. . . Our family escaped from the Frog Jump that year along with two other families from the neighborhood. When we got back from Carson City we heard that the Biker's had totally taken over the entire town.   There was absolutely no room to park a car anywhere in the Downtown area!

There were accidents and mayhem around town. Heroine, Crank, and L.S.D. was being passed around from hand to hand all over the place. One of the houses right down the street from ours was broken into and became a party house over the weekend by strangers. The roof was left sagging in because the porch posts had been kicked out!

The Angels Sing!
Surprise At The Biker Church

It doesn't seem like it would be possible, but only ten years later, the *'Biker scene'* appeared to have calmed down drastically. In the same way that the *"Jesus Movement"* impacted the *Hippy Movement*, so also, lots of *Bikers* started *"get-n saved"* and started *"Ride-n with Jesus!"* In 1982 I was attending a Church, not far from Angels Camp, that had a lot of Bikers in it. The congregation held meetings in a beautiful old one-room schoolhouse.

One Sunday morning something unbelievable happened. . .   The front of the church was full that morning, but all the way in the back, on the left side of the room, by herself, stood Margaret. . . *"The Whistler"*. . . You see, Margaret could *NOT* keep a note, so she *whistled* to the tunes during the song services. It was kind of irritating. That morning, one of the Biker-ladies was leading the song service (and as I remember, her voice was sort-a raspy and twangy, and I think she spoke with an Oklahoma, or Texan accent.) I couldn't help noticing that she had a chipped out blackish front tooth. She was a beautiful, sweet, lovely gal, but *not* someone I would recommend you tangle with. She was a *Spiritual Warrior!*

Anyway, that Sunday morning, we were all singing a simple "Halleluia Chorus" when suddenly, We heard an unbelievably beautiful fluttering voice, coming from the back of the church, right beside Margaret. No sooner had everyone heard the singing, that the Biker-lady pointed in the direction of Margaret, and blurted out; "there's an Angel!"

I think she scared the heavenly being away! The Angelic voice ceased. . . (Not to make light of it, but) I've been told that the Angels don't like the limelight, they don't like to draw a lot of attention to themselves. This is not because they are *shy*, but rather, their job is to bring glory and attention to God, and to Christ. Witnessing an

Angelic encounter like that, was an incredibly awesome thing to experience!

Without a doubt. . . Angels most definitely exist. We've witnessed them just seven or eight miles from Angels Camp in the 1980's!

FAST-TRACK, BY-PASS TO DISCOVERY > > >
Continue Here: 'Finishes' on Page 269

Angels And Demons
Michael And The Archangels

Millennialism' is based upon a presupposition that there are 'spiritual entities' (angelic beings) who exist and operate in a *'Spiritual and Heavenly Realm'*, and that these Angelic beings interact with, and are very concerned about the things that happen in the *'Earthly,'* or *'Material Realm'*

Satanic Enterprises
Total World Domination And Deception

Satan's goal has always been *'total world domination and deception'*. Throughout the entire history of the world, there have been numerous instances when Satan and his agents have managed to created alliances with particular people in order to influence the lives of not only individuals, but of entire kingdoms and empires.

The *'destiny'* of empires has no doubt influenced the destinies of multitudes of common folk throughout history. The Tower of Babel incident (mentioned in the Bible) is a good example of a movement inspired by Satan, in which a man named Nimrod built an Empire that would try to distort the relationship between mankind and their creator. The Bible tells us that Nimrod was a powerful empire builder, and that the first of his kingdoms was Babel, known later as Babylon (which was located in the geographical region known to us presently as modern day Iraq).

Satan's Demise
The Lake Of Fire. . .

Happily, 'Millennialism' teaches that Satan's demise is inevitable. At the time of Christ's return, Satan will be 'taken into custody' (so to speak) and 'jailed' for the entire duration of Christ's thousand year reign on earth. After the end of the Millennial reign 'Satan' will be released for a little while (kind of like being 'let out on bail'). . . But in *'short order,'* he will meet his final *'doom'* in a *'lake of fire'* which is called; *"Hell"*, or, *"the second death"*. The *'Millennial hope'* is not just the hope of a *'new world'* to come, but it is also a hope of a world free from Satan and his evil influences.

Now that's good news! Nevertheless, that time has not yet come, be on your guard, the Bible says that we are at war with the Devil. and the people of God are at war with Satan and his emissaries.

The Vision Of John
The Great Red Dragon

John was the last living of Jesus' 'twelve Apostles'. By the year 60 A.D., all of the other Apostles were killed because of their testimony of Jesus. Tradition says that John was thrown into a vat of boiling oil, but walked away from the ordeal unscathed. His persecutors then banished him to an Island (the Isle of Patmos) in the Mediterranean.

On the Island, John saw a series of visions relating to; the return of Christ, and the kingdom he would establish on the earth, and a 'New Heavens' and a 'New Earth' that would come after the *'Millennial Kingdom.'* John recorded the *'series of visions'* and sent them in the form of a letter to the seven main churches that were in Asia at that time.

That 'letter' from John is now known as; the book of *'Revelation'* (it's the *'last'* book of the Bible). The book of Revelation contains probably the most comprehensive Biblical collection of evidence ever showing that the ancient Christians of that time believed in *'Millennialism'* as it is understood today.

In Chapter twelve of the book of Revelation, John recorded a vision in which he saw a huge red dragon with seven heads and ten horns. The seven heads had crowns upon them. John identified the dragon as; *'Satan'*. . . the *'Devil'*. . . the *'Serpent of old'* who deceives the whole world.

In the vision, the serpent swept away '1/3rd of the stars of heaven and cast them down to the earth'. The vision went on to reveal a war in Heaven. Michael the archangel and his forces fought against the Serpent and his forces. Eventually, the *'bad guys'* were thrown out of Heaven and landed on the earth. When the Dragon realized he was 'earth bound', he got *'really'* mad and began to *'make war'* against the *'people of God'*.

A Third Of The Stars Of Heaven
The "Tail End" Of The Dragons Rule

Let's look at the statement made by John in Revelation 12 for a moment; *the stars of Heaven*. . . Now, from a Biblical perspective, the primary purpose of the *'stars'* of heaven are twofold. First, they were created to shed light on the earth. Like the sun and the moon, stars light up the night sky. Secondly, the stars are for the telling of 'time' or 'seasons'. The 'stars' are part of God's great 'Cosmic Clock'. The sun and moon tell us what time of the month or year it is, but the 'stars' help us keep track of greater periods of time. I suppose there is a 'third' reason for the *'stars'* as well, but that has to do with romance! Anyway. . .

Notice, in the passage, that the "*Devil*," who is depicted as a seven headed serpent or dragon with crowns upon each of his heads, swept away 1/3rd of 'all' of the stars of Heaven and cast them to down to the earth. . . Now catch this. . .

The Meaning of
1/3rd of the Stars of Heaven
It's All About Time. . .

According to the Millennial view of history, there will be a new set of stars made after the end of the 7000 year millennial cycle. Therefore, if *'all'* of the *'Stars of Heaven'* were taken to mean; *'all'* of the time of their existence ('7,000 years'), then '1/3rd of the *'Stars of Heaven'* would be exactly 2,333.333 years!
In other words, one third of the 7000 year Millennial Cycle. . .

What's Going On Here?
Definitely Something!

Again, There is definitely something going on here! As I looked back at the Daniel Vein I discovered three fabulous leads that were connected to John's Vision. In the very vision of 2300 evenings and mornings (Daniel 8:10) there is a reference to an evil emissary casting stars from heaven down to the ground!

246

Then in Chapter Ten (Daniel 10:12-20) there speaks of an angelic war involving Michael the Archangel (who was at war against both the "Prince of Persia" and the "Prince of Greece"). In Revelation and in Daniel, are the only two references To Stars being cast to the ground by an evil emissary and an angelic war involving the Angel Michael!

Angels and Stars
A Seven-Way Connection

Look at all of the connections between Daniel's revelations and John's vision, coupled with everything that we have seen thus far. . .

1. Michael, connected in Daniel and Revelation.

2. Angelic Warfare, connected in Daniel and Revelation.

3. Persia, (also represented by an angelic being).

4. Greece, (also represented by an angelic being).

5. $1/3^{rd}$ of the stars (which could be taken to mean $1/3^{rd}$ of 7000 years),

6. A pattern in Western History lasting 1/3rd of 7000 years starting with Alexander and the Greeks against Persia. Connected to the Prince of Persia and the *"Prince of Greece"*.

7. 2300 years (which is also connected to 1/3rd of 7000 years) ending with the restoration of the Temple mount to the Jewish people. And connected to Daniel's vision of a restoration of the Temple Sanctuary.

Now it looks obvious to me that the *'stars of heaven'* which were mentioned in John's vision, clearly refer to the 2300 year period discovered from Daniel's vision (as well as, of course, the modified 2333.333x365.25 day year period)!

All of this reveals that the struggle between the forces of the *"good angels"* against the forces of *Satan* and the *"bad angels,"* resulted in the *'political phenomenon'* that we call *'Western Civilization'*! And the *"seven heads"* of the *'Great Red Serpent'* (with seven crowns upon them), apparently represent the *'Seven Great Empires' of Western Civilization!*

These things look kind of creepy don't they? But let's just say that both visions seem obviously related to each other (the vision of

Daniel, and the vision of John), and the course of Western History is definitely a part of Mystery of the two visions. But no matter how we interpret these things, the *BIG POINT* to all of this stuff is quite obvious:

"These things produce profound evidence showing that the *Seven Thousand Year Millennial Cycle* is real, and we also *know roughly where we are* on that timeline.

PART 17

ALEX

RE-VISITED

::::: ALEXANDER EPIC SCENE :::::
'TAKE TWO!'

Let us go back now, and finish watching the 'EPIC SCENE' about Alexander 'from the top' to see what else we can learn about him and what he did, in light of what has now been revealed to us through the visions of Daniel and John. . .

Okay, go get some more pizza or something, then sit back and let's share some *'food for thought. . . The food of history'*. . .

Try to make it back here in about ten minutes, alright? I'll wait. . .

O.K. ROLE'M!

I t was a *'perfect'* spring day, sixty six degrees and sunny. A few small clusters of white cumulus clouds glisten with their proverbial *'silver linings'*. They drift nearly motionless against the brilliant blue sky overlooking the Greek landscape. The faint smell of Mediterranean Cyprus can almost be detected among a quiet symphony of other fragrances gliding in the morning breeze.

The *'Mediterranean Cyprus'* those are trees that grow straight up into the sky like pillars. They look like the heads of enormous spears jutting upwards as if they were defiantly taunting the very heavens. Like soldiers, they march serenely across the stone strewn landscape in this ancient Greek world. The year is 334 B.C.

A rush of doves flies overhead, breaking the relative silence of the morning. They've been routed from their *'place of peace'* by unfamiliar noises coming from the west. Just over the hill now, the sound crescendos to a muffled roar. It's the sound of people walking, men talking, horses, wagons, and the clatter of metal jangling.

Then, suddenly they appear! An armored throng can now be seen moving into the low-lying areas. They roll in like a flood. Before long the valley is brimming with burnished bronze, leather strappings, and the lean muscle of men and horses. It's an epic scene. It's the army of Alexander, later to be known as; *'Alexander the Great'*. He and his army are on a grand military expedition; the overthrow of the Persian Empire in the east.

Only two years earlier, Alexander became 'King of Macedonia' in place of his father Phillip, who had been assassinated by poisoning, young Alexander became king when he was only 21 years of age. No doubt Olympia had participated in the plot. Olympia was Philips first wife, and the mother of Alexander.

You see, Phillip had been taking to himself a number of other wives, and these were bearing children to him. Apparently the motive behind Olympia's involvement in the assassination plot was that she feared one of the children from Phillips *'other wives'* would inherit the throne instead of her son 'Alex'. Olympia had born a number of children to Phillip, but Alexander was *'special'*. He was the only *'sane'* child she had ever given birth to. Not only this, but she openly claimed that Alexander was of *"divine lineage"*.

When she was pregnant she had a dream that a lightning bolt struck her womb, the bolt then flashed out from her womb and spread far and wide across the horizon then disappeared. Phillip also had a dream that he was putting a 'seal' upon her womb. The "seal" was in the form of a lion's head. A prominent priest interpreted these omens, and concluded that the child (Alexander) would become a mighty warrior, and that he was the *'Son of Zeus'* (the 'chief' god of the Greek Pantheon of gods).

Besides the two stories of the dreams, Olympia also claimed that Zeus, having appeared to her in the form of a serpent, had sexual relations with her, thus making Alexander 'the son of Zeus'! This could be the reason that the shields carried by the soldiers of Alexander's army were decorated with the image of a serpent. . .

In two short years, after inheriting the throne from his father, Alexander melded the numerous Greek City States (the Macedonians, Athenians, Ionians, Thracians, and Corinthians etc.) into one united 'Greek' kingdom. He was now ready to *'take on'* Persia.

Leaving Greece in the spring of 334 B.C., when Alexander was *twenty three* years old he began his 'conquest of the Persian Empire in the east'. The clash between *'East'* and *'West'* officially began on August 25th 334 B.C. On that day, Alexander and his men first met the Persian army on the banks of the Granicus River (the Granicus was at the boundary between Europe and Asia). The Greeks were the major victors of the day, and the battle at Granicus became a harbinger for the next six years of conflict against the Persians. It was the official beginning of the end for the *'East'*.

In a short 6.4 years (*about 2,300 days*)[68] Alexander succeeded in his mission. The result was a new *'Hellenistic* (Greek) Empire' that stretched from the European continent all the way to India, and would have kept expanding the Empire, but he died shortly after the Persian victory. While he was on his deathbed, he divided up the new Empire between his four Generals.

'Party Animals'

Alexander was accustomed to throwing *'big fat parties'*. Sometimes for entertainment, they would put animals into an arena and watch them fight 'to the death'. During one of these parties, a lion and a mule were put into the same arena to fight. You can bet that no one in their right mind would ever *'wager'* on the mule, but to everyone's surprise, the mule kicked the lion in the head and killed it! Alexander, who relied heavily upon *'prophetic utterances' 'dreams'* and *'omens,'* took the incident of the lion and the mule as a *'bad omen'*. After witnessing the astonishing outcome he said; *"this is a bad omen!"* That very night Alexander took ill with a fever. He died about two weeks later.

[Just a side note: When his life was suddenly cut short, it had been exactly *230 years* since Daniel's prophecy about him (Notice the connection between Alexander and the number 23).]

One ancient historian recorded that Alexander possessed a *'peculiar'* and *'wonderfully odd'* bodily characteristic. Alexander *smelled good!* Apparently, his *'breath'* and his *'body'* emitted a pleasant *'fragrance'* that could be easily detected by those who came into close contact with him!

These are only a few of the many details and legends of Alexander's life. You can't help but love and admire the guy, and the awesome legacy he left behind. But let's interpret these things now, in the light of the revelation of the holy scriptures (namely that of the visions of Daniel and John), and even by history itself.

According to the Biblical viewpoint, *"God"* means the God of Israel. The Bible says that he alone is the only *'One True God'*. Now from that same viewpoint, the nations of this world served *'other gods'*, or *'false god's'*. The Bible says that the gods of the Gentile nations were simply *demons* who had made names for themselves in the world. They were *spirit entities*, or *angelic beings* that were part of *Satan's hierarchy*.

Now Zeus was the *"Chief"* god within the Greek Pantheon of gods. In the Bible, *Satan* is always portrayed in the form of a reptilian creature (i.e. a serpent or dragon.) Therefore, if the Greek Pantheon represented the entire hierarchy of *'false gods,'* and *Zeus* was the *chief*, then the true identity of *Zeus* would be none other than Satan himself.

Notice that *Zeus* appeared to Alexander's mother in the form of a *serpent* and inseminated her (on some level or another), thereby creating a familial connection between her child and Himself. Thus, Alexander who was proclaimed to be the *'son of Zeus'* was really the son *'Son of Satan'*. . .

Step Back, And Have A Look

Wow. . . We've certainly covered a lot of ground here! But let's step back for a moment and take another look at the *'big picture'* of what this all means. . .

Through a vision from the prophet Daniel, we have discovered a pattern of time, in the flow of history, that is connected to Alexander the great, Western Civilization, a push for Globalism. . . As well as the Six-Day-War and the restoration of the Temple Mount. We also discovered that this *"pattern of time"* is also related to the 7000 year Millennial Cycle, the culmination of the Sixth Millennium, and a result of the angelic struggle between the forces of good and evil witnessed by the Apostle John.

In all of this, we can see that a war has been raging over the destiny of the world. Whatever it was that Satan initiated when he swept away those stars with his tail is obviously connected to the things that Alexander set in motion. . . I believe that the *Seven Heads of the Satanic Dragon* coincide with the *Seven Empires* that have ruled with the resulting push for a *"One World Order"* by 'Western Man.'

This is why Alexander was passionately consumed with a dream of *'Total World*

Domination.' It was a dream that was imparted to him by his spiritual father; Zeus (Satan). So, *'like father like son'* Alexander was simply *'doing the will of his father,'* so to speak. And evidently, even beyond the scope of his own ability to understand. In all of these things, Satan has been exerting his will, and working out a specific plan for more than 2,300 years. But in 1967 something *'broke loose'* in terms of Satan's control over Jerusalem, the Temple Mount, and the Nation of Israel. Nevertheless, Satan's plan of *'global domination'* is apparently still continuing. . . but his time is short. . .

There is a great transition happening in our day. It looks like the *'restoration'* of the *'lost Kingdom of Israel'*, and the *'glorious return of Jesus Christ'* are just around the corner!

But there is plenty of tension throughout the world, and it all stems from the Middle East. The *"War On Terror"* is really just a defensive reaction against attacks launched from Moslem zealots bent on reversing the results of the 1967 Six-Day-War! All of the present day tensions in the Middle East go back to the Six-Day-War. The Moslems want Jerusalem Back (as well as everything else in the Holy Land.)

Soon after the September 11th attacks, we saw video recordings of Osama Bin Laden telling the world why he did it. He was putting pressure on America to change their policy towards Israel, in hopes of putting things back to a pre-1967 situation.

PART 18

THE

YEAR

'6000'

The 60's Generation
A Transfer of Power

So here we are, at the end of the *'Sixth Millennium.'*[(13),55]The world is a very interesting place right now. Everything is moving fast, knowledge is accelerating. . . Every time you turn around, there's a new revolution in science or technology. There are good things happening, as well as bad things. Social and political changes are taking place *'all the time'*.

But when we look back into the past century, no time seems to have been more *'revolutionary'* or *'socially'* and *'politically activated'* than in the 1960's. When you think of the *'Sixties'* you tend to think of *"sex, psychedelic drugs, rock-n-roll, rebellion against longstanding traditions, and liberalism."* The summer of 1967 was called the *"summer of love,"* but it probably would have been more accurate to call it; *"the summer of lawlessness."* The Hippies crossed all the boundaries of sexual normalcy and discretion.

I know a guy who was a cop in S.F. He used to walk his *'beat'* near Haight and Ashbury during the summer of '67'. He said *"they were like monkeys in the trees"* (referring to the mating habits!) Besides the sexual stuff, the *'Sixties'* became, as it were, a colossal *spawning ground* for an intercultural and inter-religious cross-breeding of ideas which produced a hybrid, all-encompassing *World Spirituality*.[56] It would be hard to underestimate the *ongoing* effects and influence that the *'Sixties'* generation made upon the world. . .

But there was something else happening on the other side of the world, just as the Hippies were getting high and getting naked. . . The Holy place, of the Holy land (the Temple Mount) fell back into the hands of God's original *"Holy people."* What a profoundly significant time in history!

It looks like things are being restored (things of long ago.) You know, it was back in the year 586 B.C. (during the days of the Jewish Prophet Daniel) that the King of Babylon (Nebuchadnezzar) invaded the land of Judah and *'took charge'* of Jerusalem and the Temple Mount. And ever since that time, Gentiles have *officially* been in charge there. But in 1967 everything suddenly changed. . . And now, for the first time in over 2500 years,[57] Jerusalem and the Temple Mount are again under the Jurisdiction and control of the Jewish people of Israel.

Summing Up
The GREAT BIG Puzzle

I N summarizing, I'm going to *'shoot from the hip'* (so to speak), and give you a run-down of what I believe it all means (I'm talking about the the last 300 pages or so).

My analysis won't answer everything, and I'll still have plenty more to write about in future books. But R U Ready? Here goes. . .

In my estimation, the 2300 year period of time (and subsequent patterns in the flow of history related to it) *are* that *"one third of the Stars"* mentioned by John (which actually means; $1/3^{rd}$ of 7000 years, or more specifically; $1/3^{rd}$ of the entire "7000 year Millennial Cycle.")

Somehow, Satan was able to *'secure'* a particular period of time so that he can exercise his authority in the world [this is why Satan, while tempting Jesus (Luke 4:5,6), showed Him all the Kingdoms of the World, then told Him that all of those kingdoms belonged to him.] Satan's *special time of world ruler-ship* started through Babylon, when the King of Babylon (*Nebuchadnezzar*), took possession over the headquarters of God's Kingdom (the Kingdom of the Jews, in Jerusalem.)

The "1/3rd of the Stars. ." was part of that period of time 'secured' by Satan. He intended to use the *2300 years* to implement his plan of *'Total World Domination and Deception,'* in order to create a world which would be *void* of the knowledge of the *'One True God'* (the God of Israel).

Apparently, when Satan was cast down to the earth from heaven (during the war against the forces of Michael the Archangel, and which I believe took place just before Jerusalem fell to Nebuchadnezzar in 586 B.C.), he took the remainder of world history (from that time, until the end of the sixth Millennial Day.) This is why the *'tail end'* of the '2300 years' landed around the *end* of the *Sixth Millennium of World History.*[65]

Evidently, since the *'Foundation of the World,'* the *'Seventh Millennial Day'* has been reserved for God who made it, and for his Christ. Therefore, Satan was not able to take that day, Nevertheless, the Devil's plan was to try to completely *mess up* or *destroy* the world (before flow of history could even *make it* the Seventh Millennial Day.) And with the Kingdom of God's people out of the way, Satan's plan looked like it was going to succeed unhindered. But the King of the Jews (Jesus) made a surprise appearance (just after the completion of the first *'seventh'* of the 2300 year period of time, between the Greek and Roman Empires), around the year 1 B.C. and created a resistance force (gentile believers) from among those Kingdoms who belonged to Satan. So that throughout the remaining years of Satan's *'lease'* over the Kingdom of Israel, the world would continue to see the redeeming light of the God of Israel, through those (Gentiles) who have been *'adopted in'* to Israel's Kingdom through Christ.

The Jewish people on the other hand, are seeing the wonderful restoration of their original Kingdom, and we expect that the day will be coming soon, when God will lift the blinders from off of their eyes, that they may all realize that it is Jesus who is their King. And that He is the Messiah, the very Lord God of Israel who talked to Moses face to face in the wilderness.

Who knows how all of this will *play out*, but the culmination of the 2300 year period of time lands *right* at the cusp between the Sixth and Seventh Millenniums, and personally, I believe that the official *end* of the Sixth Millennium (counting by the 360 day cycle of years) took place exactly during the Six-Day-War! The time around which, Jesus is expected to return and set up headquarters in Jerusalem where he shall reign for a *thousand years,* until the coming of the New Heavens, the New Earth, and the New Jerusalem.

Sounds dreamy, doesn't it! But <u>I</u> didn't make it up! This is what they've been talking about for two thousand years. I'm just discovering, and putting together some of the pieces of this *GREAT BIG* puzzle. . .

The End. . .
(for now)

SOURCE NOTES

REFERENCES

&

COMMENTARY

1. (page 37) Tesla Coil. Born in Croatia in the 1850's Nikolai Tesla (a Serbian), became a *'super brilliant'* electrical engineer, inventor/scientist. One of his inventions was called the "Tesla Coil." It was named of course, after him. The "Tesla Coil" is sort of a generator to produce high voltage low current type electricity. No doubt you've seen images of someone placing their hand on a big metal ball, which causes their hair to stand on end, or else, the person has continuous bolts of lightning traveling between their limbs and the Tesla coil!

2. (page 37) Leyden Jar. A device for collecting static electricity. Invented by a Dutch guy (Pieter van Musschenbroek) around 1750. It was named after the University where he worked (The University of Leiden).

Between the layer of glass, the Leyden jar is covered with metal foil on the inside, then separately on the outside of the jar. A rod coming through a cork on top of the jar touches the inside foil. When the jar is charged with static electricity, and a person touches both the outer foil and the rod, they will receive a static shock!

3. (page 39) Trompe L'oi. Pronounced "tromp-loy," is a type of painting, or, mural derived from the French words, Trompe (tramp), and L'oi (the eye), meaning; *"fool the eye."* A classic example of Trompe L'oi would be a false window, or a painting on a wall, in the shape of an arch-way which tricks your mind into thinking there is an actual arched doorway leading through the wall and into, say, a garden.

4. (page 49) Also see #26. Millennialism. Historically, there have been at least three different categories of *'Millennial teachings'* named among the Christian churches (pre-Millennial, Post-Millennial, and A-Millennial. But I have narrowed the list down to only two. I group 'Post-Millennialism' and 'A-Millennialism' together in the same category because Post-Millennialism and A-Millennialism both allegorize the Millennial reign of Christ, and neither of these two adhere to a literal 'seven thousand year cycle'. The version of 'Pre-Millennialism' (which holds to a literal seven thousand year cycle) is actually the one that I term as; 'Millennialism'.

5. (pages 49, and 107) A 7000 year cycle:
I thought Bob DeWaay did a wonderful job listing some of the early Church fathers that believed in the seven thousand year millennial cycle at; www.cicministry/scholarly/sch008.htm

6. (page 52) God rested. GENESIS: 1-2., EXODUS 20: 8-11., LEVITICUS: 19:30.

7. (pages 53, and 106) 100 years is young. ISAIAH 65:20.

8. (page 53) No night time in Jerusalem. ZECHARIAH 14:7.

9. (page 53) The General Resurrection. REVELATION 20: 11-15.

10. (page 53) New Jerusalem. REVELATION 21: 9-27.

11. (page 53) Streets of gold. REVELATION 21:21.

12. (page 53) Pearly gates. REVELATION 21:21.

13. (pages 55, and 264) A six thousand year old earth. Do some research on the names (and literary works) of guys like; Henry M. Morris, and John C. Whitcomb Jr., and also Frank R. Klassen (editor of the Reese Chronological Bible). Also see #55.

14. (page 61) Similarities between Daniel and Revelation. Some scholars place these two books in a classification called; *Apocalyptic literature.* But I have a big problem with this *'tag'* when it comes to Daniel and Revelation. Because the traditional definition of literature written in the *"Apocalyptic"* style goes something like this: *Apocalyptic literature*, is not really true. It is meant to encourage or build up the faith of those enduring times of trial and persecution, with claims of prophetic revelation (by a reputable Prophet from the past). But in reality, the revelation *and* the Author, is actually fictitious. It is really written by a well-meaning person, after-the-fact, and made to sound convincing only long enough to get the downtrodden through the hardship. The principle for this could also be compared to war-time positive propaganda agenda, designed to unify the countries resolve, and rally the national sentiments, so that victory is more certain. In other words *B.S.* equals positive victory. Or, if we get enough people to believe it (even if it's not true, we might actually win!)

15. (pages 71, and 313)   J.N. Darby's Day/Year theory. There is *some debate* going on about the influences *upon* Darby, *from* Edward Irving.   It appears (only according to my brief research) that Darby may very well have gotten at least *some* of his ideas from Irving.   But of the 'Day/Year' method of interpretation of Daniel's Prophecies, I can't tell yet.

16. (page 78) "Israel.. the center of all the nations..."   EZEKIEL 5:5

17. (page 81) The Kingdom of Israel will rule the world. DANIEL 7:18.

18. (page 82) Medes and Persian's in one night. DANIEL 5:30,31. Darius the Mede, dammed up the Euphrates River (which ran under and through the huge walls of the City of Babylon). The river dried up, and in one night, the Medes entered the City (under the walls) and took the Kingdom from Babylon!

19. (86) A Jewish Nation in the region. There are lots of people who don't like the idea of Jewish people making 'Aliyah' (the act of Ethnic Jewish people returning to live in the Land of Israel, after having been *thrust out* from that place many generations ago, by Gentile Kingdoms.)

Tons could be said about the ongoing hostilities towards the Nation of Israel, from her Arab neighbors [as well as from those Arabs who had been inhabiting the Land before the Zionists began to make *"Aliyah."* It's not my intention to try to establish defenses, or a sense of justification for the success of Zionism based on, for instance, the U.N.'s definition of human rights ["The Universal Declaration of Human Rights" which was crafted for the most part by Eleanor Roosevelt, and was adopted by the U.N. on Dec. 10th, 1948.

But my question is this: When, in history, did ethnic Jewish people (from all over the world), lose the right to return to the Land of Israel? Did they lose that right after "X" number of generations from when the Romans drove them out? The Bottom line is this; Jewish People have been moving back to their Biblical Homeland in droves since the 1800's. My intention (in GOD'S GOLD!) is to find justification for this phenomenon through the Prophetic Scriptures and through the *concept* that Israel holds a special right as a *'first born'* among the *'brother'* nations of the world.

Speaking of the *"Equal Rights of all Mankind,"* imagine Jesus *"coming back home to Israel"* and running into people there, who don't want him to be there. . . Will he submit to the U.N.'s version of Human Rights?

20. (page 101) Two teachings. . . theological landscape. Millennialism, and A-Millennialism.

21. (page 102) Alexandria Egypt. Alexandria Egypt, the fascinating, intriguing, and wonderful *'new'* city of the 'ancient world'. It was located in one of the most strategic locations for trade in the Mediterranean region.

When Alexander the Great conquered the various regions of the Persian Empire, he established new *'Greek'* cities along the way. Each city was named *'Alexandria'* (after himself). There were thirteen Alexandrian cities in all. The purpose of the Alexandrian cities (besides military or commercial considerations) was for the promotion of the Greek culture, known as; *'Hellenism'* or the *'Greek way.'*[32]

The most famous and influential of these was 'Alexandria Egypt'. Established in the year 333

B.C., it is said that Alexander marked out the location of the city himself. The legend says that in a dream, Alexander received the plans for the 'layout' of the city. The next morning he could not find any lime (chalk) to mark out the boundaries of the city, so he used grain. The analogy is that to establish the boundaries with crushed rock would imply that the city would become just another empty monument of stone, but to lay out the foundational boundaries with grain implied that the city would be a city that would continue to spawn reproducing seeds of the Greek culture.

'Alexandria Egypt' became home to one of the 'seven wonders of the ancient world'. This was a massive light house estimated at around 450 feet high (that's 150% as tall as the statue of liberty). The beam of light that emanated from this massive towering edifice is believed to have been seen 200 miles away. Alexandria became home to a huge library, which possessed the entire body of works from every known Philosopher of Greece (not to mention thousands of other literary works of antiquity). The library was in existence for more than three centuries before *and* three centuries after the time of Christ. Some of the things you could find in Alexandria Egypt were drawings of a machine that utilized steam propulsion. Also, vending machines that worked off of Greek coins were found in the ruins of this great city. These types of things are commonplace today, but they were already 'conceived of' and probably already in use in ancient Alexandria.

JESUS OF NAZERETH

It is believed that Jesus of Nazareth lived in Alexandria Egypt during some of his childhood years. According to the Biblical account of his early life (Matthew, Chapter 2: 1-23.) states that Mary and Joseph fled to Egypt with the child Jesus, in order to escape an attempt on his life by King Herod. In those times, if you were a Jew living in Egypt, you probably lived in Alexandria, where there was a very large Jewish community.

22. (pages 102, and 103) Platonism. The philosophy of Plato, or philosophies and doctrinal views rooted in the same vein of thought influenced and outlined by the teachings of Plato.

23. (page 102,) Plato. The first Greek Philosopher was a man named Thales. Today, he is known as; the 'father of science'. Starting with Thales, a fermentation of thought began among the Greeks. And by the end of a two hundred year-long evolutionary development of *'philosophical inquiry,'* the three greatest Philosophers of their history emerged. These were; Socrates, **Plato**, and Aristotle (in that order). Socrates became Plato's teacher, and Plato became Aristotle's teacher.

The Greek philosophical movement produced a *'golden age'* of Greek culture known as; *'Hellenism'* or, the *'Greek Way,'* and the fully developed *'fruit'* from this unique Philosophical movement came to full maturity just as Alexander the Great stepped onto the world scene. As a youth, Alexander's 'personal tutor' was none other than *'Aristotle'* himself (not to belittle **Plato** [nor Socrates either for that matter], but Aristotle has been regarded as the greatest Greek Philosopher of them all). Aristotle continued to be Alexander's lifelong friend as well.

Having been a student of the renowned teacher Aristotle (in the tradition of Socrates and **Plato**), it became abundantly clear to Alexander, that the *'Greek way'* was the *'best way'*, so he was eager to spread the 'good news' of the 'Greek way' to the ends of the earth.

24. (page 106) Jesus' use of allegory. JOHN 4:14.

25. (page 106) The Apostle Paul and Allegory. The passage in GALATIONS 4:21-31. Shows us a good example of the Apostle Paul's use of allegory.

26. (page 107). Also see #2.(page37) Spin-offs. Two kinds of Christian teaching. When I convey the idea that there have been basically only two kinds of teachings or views within the historical scope of Christianity, (Millennialism and A-Millennialism), I meant just that. But some would contend that there have been many more than only these two. To give you an example, there is view called: 'Post-Millennialism', the adherents of which are no small number of persons. Nevertheless, Post Millennialism is a prime example of what I meant when I said that there have been "spin offs and modifications to both streams of Christian teaching".

I would place Post Millennialism as a sub category of A-Millennialism because it doesn't teach that there is a literal thousand year period on earth when Christ will reign from a literal place on earth (Jerusalem). In other words, Post Millennialism allegorizes the material and literal hopes of the original Christian message.

On the other hand, There was a certain teacher in the early centuries of Christianity (unfortunately I can't confirm his name or the details of his life. His name may have been Nestorian?). Anyway, the man was 'Millennial' in his teaching (at least in regards to the literal return of Jesus Christ to this earth). But the problem was that he taught that Jesus was coming back not to Jerusalem, but rather to this teachers own home town (somewhere in what is now modern day Turkey).

This type of modification to the traditional Millennial teaching is very similar to something I encountered while talking to a Mormon friend a few years ago. When we were comparing our beliefs with one other, and discussing the subject of our common hope of Christ's literal return to this earth someday, the Mormon woman explained (quite emphatically) that Jesus was not going to be 'touching down' on the Mount of Olives near Jerusalem. But rather, he will be 'touching down' somewhere in Missouri U.S.A.!

27. (page 108) The Chosen Nation.
DEUTERONOMY 14:2., EXODUS 19:5.

28. (page 108) A Blessing for all Nations.
GENESIS 12:2-3., 22:18.

29. (page 108) To the Jew first.. ROMANS 1:16, ROMANS 2:5-11, [Notice that the Apostle Paul clearly holds the Jewish people in a position of preeminence (from God's perspective), yet immediately following, in verse eleven, he points out that God is no respecter of persons. In other words, though the Jews are preeminent as a specially chosen people, they are not immune to God's judgment in terms of wrongdoing in light of the laws of God written upon the hearts of all men (men and women). In fact, those who had the laws of God in writing, may very well be held even *more* accountable. . . ROMANS 3:1-2.

Since both Jews and Gentiles alike (according to the Apostle Paul) have sinned and have fallen short of God's ideals, they must then all-together seek the mercies of God for their justification before him. . . On the other hand, God has still retained the right to show (unusual) mercy to whom-so-ever he chooses. And in holding to his merciful nature, we can probably safely assume, that when he shows *unusual mercy* to one person over another, it is probably because the results of his actions of grace will work towards the good of the most! Furthermore (from the teachings of the Old and New Testaments), it looks quite obvious that God's general intentions are to show mercy to all mankind, and in a way that does not nullify the promises of his mercy (formerly made) to the people of Israel (even in spite of their unbelief or rebellion against him). Nor is his favor *necessarily* based upon merit (on the part of either Jew *or* Gentile) even though we know that God is a faithful rewarder of those who do good.

The bottom line. . . 1. God is merciful.
2. Always be reverent of God, but don't presume upon his mercy (In other words; "don't p&%* him off!.") 3. Be careful how you judge another. . . Seek his favor, because he is merciful. . . Even to Gentiles, and even to Israel!   Wow!

30. (page 108) Unbroken promises. ROMANS 11: 25-36. Paul explained a certain mystery (about the Nation of Israel) to the believer's in Rome. He told them that a temporary hardening has taken place within the Nation of Israel, and that it's duration is contingent upon a certain future time or condition in relation to the Gentile Nations. . . This is only speculation, and I can't elaborate upon it at the moment, but I believe this passage possibly means; until the gentile ruler-ship over Jerusalem is finally ended. Or, essentially, the mystery which takes in to account things like the 2300 years, and the Six-Day-War, and the present day restoration of Israel's place in their ancient Land. . .

31. (page 109) Israel: A stubborn people. EXODUS 32:9-14., DUETERONOMY 9:6., DUETERONOMY 10:15,16., ACTS 7:51-60.

32. (page 132) The Greek Way. Another term for Hellenism. Apparently, the term; "The Greek Way" was coined by Edith Hamilton, in her 1930 book by the same name (The Greek Way). Regarded as the greatest woman Classicist, Edith was a German-American Educator, Author, who wrote extensively about the Classic Greco-Roman era.   She also wrote a book (among others) titled; The Roman Way.

33. (page 135) Charlemagne. Check him out on the web.

34. (141) The Maccabean Surprise. I'll probably deal with this, in another book. Perhaps the title will be; MORE GOD'S GOLD!

35. (154) Mark Twain. ("King of Irreverence"… "Champion of Humanism"… And a major forerunner of "Global Liberalism"). Much could be said about ole Mark Twain. His real name was Samuel Langhorne Clemens. Mark Twain may have been the first person to invent *"standup comedy."* He rented opera halls in San Francisco and charged admission to hear his lectures (as would do, perhaps say, a world traveling Scientist, bringing back news from an expedition to some place far and wide). But Twain was doing so, as a witty or cynical "spoof."

It appears Mark Twain was following in the footsteps of the Greek (Cynic) Philosopher Diogenes of Sinope, who enjoyed making sport of Plato, while he was, with great seriousness, lecturing [in what, by modern day comparisons (1800's) would be the equivalent of an opera house.] I've much more to say about *'Diogenes'* in a possible next edition of God's Gold. Or, get ahold of my up-and-coming book: "The Alexandrian Conspiracy. . . "

36. (pages 185, 186, and 190) Ancient Wisdom, Dangerous Things. LEVITICUS 19: 31. Not necessarily *all*, but perhaps *much* of the Ancient

Wisdom (i.e. the wisdom of Pharaoh's Magicians, or the Babylonian Astrology) seems to have been acquired through occult means, with the help of spiritual entities, not associated with the "One True God of the Bible." This poses a *big* problem for a person who desires to study the mysteries, and Wisdom of the ancients. I believe there is a way to process some of it, without becoming drawn away into its occult or Pagan vortex. I plan to deal with this dilemma in another book entitled *"The Alexandrian Conspiracy"*..

37. (pages 186, and 190) A 'Holy" and "Clean" kind of numerology. Some of the obvious examples of Biblical accounts containing numerological meaning would be the cases involving the number 40. i.e. During the flood of Noah it rained 'forty' days and nights. Or when Moses didn't eat for 'forty days'. Or when the spies checked out the Land of Canaan 'forty days, and how the Children of Israel wandered in the wilderness 'forty years'.

In the New Testament, Jesus fasted 'forty days. Then there are all the cases where the number twelve is referenced i.e. "the twelve tribes of Israel", the "Twelve Apostles", and the 'twelve' gates of the City of *"New Jerusalem."* Again, we have a case where there are a special number of 'chosen ones' in the book of Revelation (144,000).

One hundred and forty four equals 12 x 12 x 1000. These numbers are pretty 'cut and dried'.

Now it's not my purpose to try to explain the meaning of these numbers at this time, but only to point out the fact that there are plenty of examples of numerological phenomenon in the Bible itself. Aside from these examples, there are plenty of other cases which are more complicated. Especially those related to things like the measurements and proportional dimensions of the Tabernacle and Temples of the Lord.

The building specifications of the Tabernacle listed in EXODUS 25: 1- 27:19. were given to Moses straight from the Lord, and they hold numerological significance. Be assured that these dimensions were not arbitrary. The dimensions and specifications for Solomon's Temple listed in 2 CHRONICLES 3:1-5:14. were divinely inspired as well. 1 CHRONICLES 28:11-19. Gives an account of how the Lord gave King David all of the plans for the design, dimensions, and details of the Temple that his son Solomon built. The entire account of how the Temple came about is found starting in Chapter 17:1 of the book of 1 CHRONICLES, and ending at the 22nd verse of Chapter 7 in the book of 2 Chronicles). Again, in the book of EZEKIEL Chapter 40:1 thru 42:20 there is a detailed account given by the Prophet Ezekiel for a Temple which has not been built yet.

Many believe these measurements have numerological significance, yet will they will also be the literal dimensions of a future Temple which will be built on the ancient Temple Mount site where the Moslem 'Dome of the Rock' Mosque is presently located. One should have no trouble finding a plethora of books and sources online that deal with the numerological meanings behind the various Tabernacle and Temple measurements, but be careful, not everyone's analysis is correct.

When it comes to numerological sites on the internet there's plenty of 'weird' stuff out there as well!]). The Tabernacle and Temple measurements are only one example of where we find cases of numerological phenomena in the Bible. Another reference is in 2 KINGS 5:1-19 where Elisha the Prophet told the Naaman (the commander of the army of king of Syria) to dip himself in the Jordan river "seven times". Why 'seven' times?

Another example of mathematical (or numerological phenomenon) is where Elisha wanted a double portion of the Spirit of God that was on Elijah (2 Kings 2:9-10.). Read all of the accounts of Elijah and Elisha from I Kings 17:1 thru 2 Kings 13:21., and you will find that every miracle that Elijah performed, Elisha did twice, two times or double. Read the stories yourself and see if you can see the 'double portion' pattern. It is interesting to note that the dividing line in the history of Israel was during the days of Elijah and Elisha.

Greek Style Geometry
The Geometric Form

'The Triangle, Square, and Circle'

The primary geometrical expression for the Pagan Gentile world would be the Triangle, Square, and Circle. These were the foundation of the Greek Philosophical system that produced Western Civilization. The Greek philosophers noticed that everything in the tangible three dimensional universe can be reduced down to three primary geometric forms; The Triangle, the Square, and the Circle.

This structural basis of thinking had to be grappled with by the fledgling Christian community. Was the *"source"* of the Pagan wisdom from the True God of the Bible or was it an inspiration from the Demons? [Much, much more could be said about this subject, and I will go into this subject much deeper in another book: "The Alexandrian Conspiracy"].

In the New Testament book of Romans, the Apostle Paul explained that the attributes of God can be clearly seen through the things which he has made (the universe). Everything that was 'made' in the material universe possesses three dimensional geometric 'form'. The "three form" revelation became the basis for explaining the triune nature of God. The New Testament goes to great lengths to explain the mystery of how things that were once *"un-clean"* are now made *"clean"* by Faith through Christ. The Gentiles were "un-clean, certain foods were "un-clean. Somewhere in one of the gospels the author said that Christ proclaimed all foods clean.

In the book of Acts Peter received a clear message from the Lord that he should associate with certain Gentiles who had formerly been considered "un-clean. In my up-and- coming book; The "Alexandrian Conspiracy" I'll explain why the Greek system of Geometry came directly from

Satanic origins, yet it can now be considered "clean food" for the believer in Jesus Christ.

40. (page 201) The Day of Rest. See # 1.

41. (pages 203, and 205) The Star Of David. [In this reference I deal with some of the debate regarding the origins of the Star of David, and reveal some pretty cool stuff that seems to connect the design directly to King David himself.]

Some people claim that the beautiful emblem called the *"Star of David"* was originally an *'occult'* symbol, and that somehow it was adopted by the Jewish people during the *'Middle Ages.'* There are also allegations that suggest the *'Star'* was a symbol of an Egyptian God named *'Remphan'* and was related to the bovine deity (whom the children of Israel worshiped while they were in the wilderness during the time of Moses). I don't like the *'occult origin'* hypothesis because it seems to *'fly in the face'* of the idea that supposes God is behind the restoration of the Jewish people to their ancient homeland today, and that he has been behind the formation of the Modern day nation of Israel. Either way, the Star symbol seems to fit perfectly with the uniquely Jewish answer for the origins of the universe (not to mention that of the destiny of the world according to the first century believers as well).

For whatever it's worth, I propose yet another consideration (below) which supports the idea that King David himself holds the *'copyright'* or *'trade mark'* to this beautiful emblem. There is a Biblical account in the book of 2 Samuel (chapter 23 verses 8 thru 39) which reveals an interesting numerological insight that I believe connects the six pointed star directly to King David. The Biblical account that I am referring to deals with King David and his 'mighty men of war'.

We've probably all heard about David's courageous confrontation against the nine foot tall Philistine giant named Goliath. As a young man, David killed Goliath with a simple sling and stone, and finished up the job by cutting off the giants head with his own sword (the sword of Goliath). After this courageous feat David became the Hero of Israel, and eventually became their King. The Bible records that in the upper echelon of David's Army there was a hierarchy of warriors called "David's mighty men". These were men of extreme valor and who were found to be the most brave and loyal of all his soldier/friends. If David had a Facebook page, the pictures of these men would be the first ones posted on his list of *'friends.'*

There are two places in the Bible that list the names of David's mighty men. These two places also tell us a little bit about the various ranks that these men held within the upper echelon of David's military hierarchy. In the scholarly world of Biblical exegesis there is debate as to the actual number of men who were included in the company of David's mighty men (and also debate regarding their names as well). Nevertheless, in 2 Samuel 23: 8-39 it clearly states that there were tells us that there were 37 men in all.

The passages mention three distinct men of exceptional bravery, then one man greater than those three. After him there was another man who was ranked less than the three, but greater than a group of men called the *"thirty."* Now, If we add David's top General, 'Joab', and King David himself (as leader of all), then we arrive at a number of elite soldiers in David's upper echelon (David included) consisting of thirty seven men in all. Together they would form a framework or organizational structure that would look like this:

David at the top and center (the mightiest of all).

Next, David was surrounded by the top six men. These were the *'super tough guys'* (his *'inner circle'*)...

Next, David and the *'six'* were themselves surrounded again by the *'thirty'*...

Thirty seven in all!

Now comes the *'fun'* part... David and his inner circle can be compared to the six pennies that surround the first penny (represented by David himself). In other words; the seven pennies represent David and his top six men.

King David and his top six men

The seven pennies (above) look sort of like a *"Star of David,"* but let's keep going with this... Let's keep adding pennies to the configuration until it *'unmistakably'* forms the shape of a traditional *'Star of David.'* As we keep adding pennies, we will find that it takes exactly 30 more pennies to form the primary configuration of the *"Star of David"* 37 in all... WOW!

King David and his "Mighty Men"

I don't know about you, but think this is awesome! Here we have a Biblically based numerological connection between the geometrical form of the traditional *Star of David*, coinciding with the story of *King David and his "Mighty Men"*

42. (page 208) Harmony in creation. The laws that Moses gave the people of Israel covered all areas of life. Rules of conduct about how masters should treat their servants, versus how servants should treat their masters. There were laws telling them how to treat the soil and how to treat the fruit trees that grew in the soil. He even gave them laws about how the Israelites should treat baby birds in the wild!

43. (page 209) Contract between a master and his servant. EXODUS 21:1-11.

44. (page 209) Agricultural laws. LEVITICUS 25:1-22.

45. (page 210) The Jubilee Year. LEVITICUS 25: 8-13.

46. (page 212) The 'ten day week' of the French Revolution.
Go to:
www.webexhibits.org/calendars/calendar-french.html

47. (page 212) Failure of the ten day week. Unfortunately, in regards to the sick animals and people, I can't find that source at the moment, but I'm almost positive that I read it in a book authored by *Ivan Panin*. Mr. Panin was a pioneer in the field of numbers in the Bible. Nevertheless, The so called 'Republican Calendar' (which was based on the number ten) was a philosophical sham! It's ironic that it only lasted ten years.

48. (page 212) Major national developments every 500 years. You see, when Moses delivered the people out of Egypt, he did not appoint a king over them (as was the custom of all other nations). The Lord wanted them to be different from other people... He didn't want his people to be under that kind of oppressive and controlling system.

The Lord Himself wanted to be their king! Nevertheless, Moses predicted that the day would eventually come when the people would ask for a king (in order to be like all the other nations). So he laid out the ground rules for them, so they would have them in that day (Deuteronomy 17:14-20). Well, the day finally came, and the people asked for a king (so they would *'fit-in'* with the *"crowd"* of all the other nation's round about them).

Again, these things happened 500 years after the establishment of the system that Moses put in place (1 Samuel 8:1-22). Then, 500 years after the beginning of the establishment of the kings of Israel, came the rule of Babylon over Israel's kingdom, which is prophetically described by Moses in Deuteronomy Chapter 28:1 thru chapter 29:29. And 500 years after Babylon came the *"King of Israel himself: Jesus Christ!"* Many believe that Moses seems to alluding to Christ in Deuteronomy 18:18.

49. (page 214) A priestly order. EXODUS 28:1-30:38.

50. (page 215) Solomon's Temple. David initiates and prepares to build the Temple, but gives the job of building it to Solomon I KINGS 5:1-9:14., I CHRONICLES 17:1-29:30. Solomon begins the work of building the Temple. Hence, it is called; "Solomon's Temple". 2 CHRONICLES 1:1-7:22.

51. (page 215) Zadok. 2 SAMUEL 8:17., I KINGS 1:7,8,32-45. I CHRONICLES 24:3.

52. (page 215) The Babylonian Captivity. CRONICLES 36:15-21. outlines a summary of the circumstances leading up to the Babylonian captivity of the people of Judah.

53. (page 215) Ezra. NEHEMIAH 8:4-12. Ezra the High Priest of the post captivity Temple in Jerusalem taught the people reading from the Law of Moses. The key here is that he caused them to know the meaning of the words, which caused the people to weep. Obviously there had been a language barrier between teacher (priest) and pupil (average Jewish person). Perhaps the same thing had happened in ancient Israel that later happened in Western Christian culture during the 13th to 14th centuries.

The official Priestly language was Latin, but the common languages (i.e. English) were considered vulgar. When John Wycliffe produced an English version around 1384 the seeds of major Christian revival began to sprout. One hundred and twenty years after Wycliffe died the Reformation exploded in Europe. Like Nehemiah, Wycliffe caused the people to understand the meaning of the Biblical Text.

54. (page 216) Herod's Renovation. MARK 13:1-2., LUKE 21:5-6., MATTHEW 24:1-2. The Temple renovation by Herod the Great was in progress at the time of Christ, Jesus predicted it's destruction. The building stones were beautiful and huge!

55. (page 264) The end of the *'Sixth Millennium.'* See # 13.

56. (page 265) World Spirituality. The New Age Movement is a conglomeration of shared Spiritual experiences and teachings from many different traditions (i.e. from native American medicine men, to Shamans in Siberia, to Australian Aborigines, to Buddhist and Hindu monks, as well scudo Jewish and Christian Mysticism). I believe that the term 'New Age Movement' would be better termed; 'World Spirituality'.

57. (page 265, 314, and 324) Restoration after twenty five hundred years! Nebuchadnezzar took Jerusalem and the land of Judah in 586 B.C. From that date in history until the Six-day-War there were around 2553 years.

58. (page 217) Enoch. GENESIS 5:21-24, HEBREWS 11:5.

59. (page 130, but especially page 314) 334 B.C. The year Alexander's began to conquer. The actual book in which I first noticed the year of Alexander's conquest, actually quoted the year as being 333 B.C. That is because the older books on the subject miss calculated for the year "one" assuming that there was a year "0" (zero). There of course is no year "zero", and the actual year of the beginning of Alexander's conquest is 334 B.C.

60. (page 316) Hanukkah! When I made my initial discovery of the three way connection between Alexander, the Six-Day-War, and 2,300 years, I'm convinced that it was during Hanukkah. I discovered the connection during the Christmas transition. My wife and son had flown to the Mainland to visit family for Christmas and New Year's. I'm just not sure which *day* during the eight day celebration It happened.

This is very meaningful to me, because of the obvious primary connection between the '2,300 evening and morning vision' and the celebration which is now called Hanukkah. It's very special and fitting to think that the Lord would reveal that connection to me on that particular Holiday!

61. (page 320) The Longest day. JOSHUA 10:1-15.

62. (page 31) Prayed 'in the Spirit.' Opening our mouth so God can fill it. PSALMS 81:10., JUDE 1:20, and especially; [I CORINTHIANS 14:14,15., (in the context of: I CORINTHIANS 12:1-thru-14:40.)]. These passages explain the *Gift* of God's Spirit, in the life of a *'Gifted Believer."*

63. (page 24) Doing nothing at all. In their minds, we're not supposed to do anything. . . And God does everything! When it comes to "opening our mouth so God can fill it" (referring to Psalms 81:10) their perception seems to be that it's a person's job to do nothing more than give an involuntary 'YAWN'. . . (in other words, you aren't even supposed to *trying* to 'open up your mouth) And at that point, while our jaws are temporarily and uncontrollably locked in the *"open position,"* God fills our mouth with all of the good things that come from his hand! Don't misunderstand, God *'starts'* everything. He is the *'Great Initiator,'* he is also the *"Perfecter"* (finisher) of our Faith. But if the seed of Faith has sprouted in your heart, you must give all that it is requiring of you i.e. courage, intelligence, strength etc., or you run the risk of 'losing out' on your reward from God!

I think the *'open mouth thing'* is better interpreted by something we might see in one of those nature films, where there are about eight little chicks crowded in a tiny nest, all of them stretching their necks as far as they will go, their mouths seem to open wider than is actually possible! They are doing *all* that they possibly can, to fill their mouths and supply the demand that their teensy-weensy lives require! Yet, they are helpless without the aid of the parent bird.

So also, in the *'Walk of Faith'*, we simply do *all* that we can do (which sometimes is more than we may think we are capable of, but at the same time, it may also be surprisingly less as well. *It's a tricky thing!*). And it shouldn't be an *oppressive thing* either (Jesus said that the burden of Faith is not a back breaker). So we can cheer up. In this kind of relationship, while we are giving it our all, God will be doing for us what we couldn't possibly do for ourselves. And *that* is when the biggest reward is discovered!

64. (page 24) Ask Not, Have Not. JAMES 4:2.

65. (page267) the *end* of the *Sixth Millennium of World History*. I can't prove it, and it is not really the premise of this book, but I hold a personal belief, that the Six-Day-War marked the official *end* of **exactly** six thousand years of world history, calculating from the original '360 day' cycle of years. Something to think about.

66. (page 170) Memorizing the Proverbs of Solomon. There is a collection of exactly 374 proverbs by King Solomon, recorded in the Book of Proverbs, from chapter 10:1 thru chapter 22: 18. I call this collection; 'The *Best* of Solomon.' At the conclusion of the collection (Proverbs 22: 17-21), there is a summarizing statement, which essentially tells the reader that they should memorize it.

I'd like to think that Solomon's *gift of wisdom* was actually intended to become a sort of a *national literacy* and *educational reform program* within the Kingdom. The collection was, no doubt, meant to become the standard elementary educational curriculum for the sons of Israel. I suppose the priests, and Levites must have been, for the most part, of course, necessarily literate. And there was *a lot* for them to *know about*, *write about*, and *study*. They were the *'teachers'* of

Israel, and their job was to be the 'white collar' *paper pushers* of the day.

But I'm thinking that the collection of Solomon's 374 Proverbs could have probably been memorized by anybody. It was *blue collar* wisdom that could bring the whole nation to a new level of intelligence and righteousness. Rabbis supposedly memorized huge section of the Torah (the books of Moses, the first 5 books of the Old Testament). But again, they took on the job of the Priests and Levites. That was their job, but the Proverb collection is *streamlined, simple, and straightforward*. It can be grasped and learned by anyone.

I memorized most of the proverbs, by writing them down on 3x5 cards. I developed a system where I could memorize *'one proverb per day,'* followed by a simple maintenance program to keep them fresh in my mind. But I must confess, I've gotten rusty, but for years, I could rattle many of them off like a machine gun. Or, I'd ask someone to give me a number between, say, 1 and 200 then I would tell them the proverb.

It's been a quest of mine for years, but there were pitfalls that made the system collapse from time to time, like neglecting the simple maintenance program, or not having the 3x5's on hand etc. Sometimes the cards would get all mixed up and. . . blah, blah, blah, . . . Anyway, I think I've worked out all of the major *bugs* from the system, and received some special wisdom on how to more effectually memorize the Wisdom of Solomon. . .

At *this very moment*, I'm working on a *NEW BOOK* which will have the complete collection of 374 Proverbs, *and* the memorization system, all together in a paperback book, that can easily be carried around anywhere. No more losing or mixing up 3x5 cards. This will be an enormous step up from the previous 3x5 card system. *EVERYTHING WILL BE IN THE BOOK!* With this book, virtually anyone should be able to memorize the 374 Proverbs of Solomon in about a year's time.

The book is titled: ***"The Best Of Solomon,"*** 'Memorize 365 Proverbs of Solomon in 1 Year' (by Mike Darby) and will be available soon enough!

67. (page 117) Planet 'X'. The "Titius-Bodes law" (discovered around 1750) showed that there is a proportional pattern among the six (then known) planets, in terms of their orbital distances from the sun.

If we divide the distance between the Sun and Saturn into 100 parts, we will find that Mercury lands on the *fourth* part out from the sun. Next, Venus lands at 4+(3) or,7 parts away from the sun. Then the Earth, at 4+(6) or, 10 parts from the Sun, and Mars lands at 4+(12). The original number *'three'* doubles with each new planetary position away from the sun (i.e. 3,6,12,24, 48, 96 etc.) Saturn is located at 4+96 which is of course 100 parts. Now, Uranus was later discovered right where it was supposed to be, at 4+192, but there was a *'mystery gap'* between Mars and Jupiter. . . The *"Mystery Gap"* led to a *'hunt'* for the missing planet. The *'hunt'* was successful, when someone discovered a planet on the predicted path between Jupiter and Mars. . . . or so it seemed.

The newly discovered planet was named; *'Ceres,'* but years later, Astro-scientists concluded that it was not actually a planet. Instead, it was the largest meteor within a *'belt'* of meteors (the meteor belt). Ceres has been dubbed; a *'Dwarf Planet.'*

Pluto fits closely into the following expected position after Uranus, but Neptune is *way* out of place. Neptune's position led to the discrediting of the law by some scientists, but the point in all of this, is simple. To me, it looks quite obvious that a pattern exists (or existed) in the solar system, and that something catastrophic happened which changed things a little bit. Perhaps Neptune is a miss placed planet, and the 'asteroid belt' is only the remains of a planet (planet "x") which used to orbit on the fifth line out from the sun.

One (down to earth) way in which we could describe this conundrum of astronomical chaos, would be the theory of "'wear and tear' beauty within aging classical ruins" (my own theory.) Take an ancient statue for instance. Originally, the statue was perfect in proportion and therefore beautiful. But after an arm was broken of here, and a nose there (as well as some weathering in different places), the statue is as beautiful as ever, because our mind and imagination fills in the missing parts. The beauty can still be appreciated!

So also, the beauty of the order and position of the planets, can still be appreciated through the Titius-Bodes Law. And evidence of a great astronomical catastrophe backs up my hypothesis about the change-over between an original 360 day year, and the present 365.25 day year.

68. (page 256) 2300. An interesting note; I need to do some further research, but it appears as though there were exactly 2300-2333 days from the onset of Alexander's mission, and the establishment of the last Alexandrian City (Alexandria Eschata). This is significant, because it is just one more connection about the proportion of 2300 (which really implies the number 2333.333).

Another example of this phenomenon can be seen during the time frame between the beginning of the Six-Day-War, and the next big war in Israel (the Yom-Kippur War) which began on Oct 6th 1973, and lasted until Oct 25th 1973. The period of time between the start of the Six-Day-War, until the end of the 73 War was really close (if not exactly) 2333.333 days!

GOD'S GOLD EXTRAS

This section is dedicated to stuff that I wanted to put into the main body of the book, but thought it necessary to *cut out* instead. Go ahead and check it out, if you like.

Deleted Scenes

CUT 1
The Maccabean Revolt, and the Three-Way-Connection

Some Biblical Critics suggest that the book of Daniel was really just a fabrication, written after-the-fact (during the days of the Maccabees) to stir up and encourage, with *Apocalyptic fervor,* the hopes of those weary and persecuted resistors of Antiochus. . .

Now, it's quite obvious that Daniel's vision predicted the events of the "Maccabean Revolt". Therefore, many Theologians and Biblical Scholars believe that the vision was completely fulfilled around the middle of the second century B.C..

On the other hand, some believe that the vision may yet hold another, *'greater'* fulfillment. And that Daniel's vision of 2300 Evenings and Mornings" may also refer to a period of time lasting 2,300 years. . . [15] In that same vein of thinking (2,300 days equals 2,300 years), I began considering the events of the 1967 Six-Day-War in Israel.

During that War, the Nation of Israel regained possession of the ancient Temple Mount site, which had been lost to them for more than 2,500 years (starting when King Nebuchadnezzar of Babylon invaded the land of Judah, and the City of Jerusalem in 586 B.C.[57]). So I subtracted 2,300 years from the Six-Day-War and I got 334 B.C. At this point I began to wonder if anything significant may have taken place in that year. There happened to be a book in my living room about the history of the Jews (which I had previously checked out of the campus Library.) Anyway, I opened the book to search for the year 334 B.C. and to my surprise the book happened to fall open right to a page that showed the date: "334 B.C."[59] Huh?

And there it was! . . . Alexander and the Greeks began to conquer Persia in 334 B.C. Wow!!!

"From the exact year that Alexander began to conquer the Persians until the Six-Day-War there were exactly 2,300 years!"

CUT 2
The
Three-Way-Connection
And Hanukkah

My Initial Discovery!
"Happy Hanukkah"... An Amazing Connection Between Daniel, Alexander, and the Six-Day-War

I couldn't believe it! Daniel's vision started out with a symbolic representation of the Greeks (typified by a male goat), who were conquering the Medo-Persians (typified as a ram). Then, at the *end* of the vision, a promise was given about a *'restoration'* of the Sanctuary of the Temple in Jerusalem after 2,300. . . And wham! There's the Gold!. . .

2,300 years after Alexander and his army began to conquer the Persian's, the Ancient Temple Mount Site was restored to the Jewish people!

Wow! There was definitely gold in this vein of thinking. . . God's gold. The riches of his wisdom and revelatory knowledge. This 2,300 year "Three-Way-Connection" between *Daniel, Alexander,* and the Six-Day-War was like finding a pocket of gold right at the surface of the ground! It was so-o-o obvious!

But there was something else that made this discovery even more special to me... Something that really "blew me away". It has to do with the date that I discovered the *"three way connection. . ."*

   . . . It was during Hanukkah![60]

CUT 3
Geometry

The foundation of a triangle is its base. Six of them fit together perfectly into a kind of circle (hexagon). If we make an equilateral triangle so that its base is 'seven', we will find that the height of the triangle comes <u>really</u> <u>close</u> to six. I have a hunch that this ratio is in some way connected to the mystery of the six-seventh relationship. Now they say that "close only counts in horse shoes and hand grenades", but sometimes, when we think we see something (like a pattern), even though it's not 'perfect', but really close..., it is probably worth further investigation. I'll give you another example of this sort of thing. Let's make a triangle with a foundational base of "1" and an equal height of "1". Next, arrange the triangles next to each other in a circle (sort of like the "Millennial Pizza"). Seven of these triangles fit together almost perfectly!

CUT 4
The Number Seven

A COSMOLOGY OF SEVEN TOOLS

There is yet another way in which we can see the unique attributes of the number seven. It's a cosmology of 'tools'. This cosmology was discovered by the author of 'Day Six' (that's me), and as far as I know, no one else has come up with this cosmology. I like to call it: 'The Seven Primary Tools'. Here's how it goes: There are seven primary tools from which are derived all other tools. Within the seven, one tool is unique among the other six. The lineup goes like this;

1. the sword,

2. the shield,

3. the staff,

4. the cord (rope),

5. the cup,

6. the hammer (or stone).

7. The lamp (or fire), which is the unique one among the other six

There is are opposite characteristics within six of the seven tools. . .

The *sword* cuts or divides
(separates).

The *shield* covers and keeps things out
(separates).

The *staff* holds things apart
(separates).

As opposed to:

The *cord* binds
(holds things together).

The *cup* holds or contains things
(holds things together).

The *hammer* forces things together
(holds things together).

Then, the unique tool. . .

The *Lamp* (or *fire*) is just plain different. . .

The challenge goes forth! Try to find any 'tool' that doesn't fall into the category of one of these seven, *or* is not a combination thereof. . . Now someone may well say; "what about a wheel, a fulcrum, or a screw"? Yes, these are all unique tools, and they are on a higher level of complexity and but still be reduced to one (or a combination) of the seven primary tools. The wheel (and it's axel) are actually related to the staff (and possibly the shield. Just take a look at a wagon wheel. The fulcrum is obviously the staff and stone. The screw is clearly a combination of the sword and the cord and staff, because it cuts, and binds things together, yet it is definitely like a staff as well.

CUT 5
Jerusalem

All right, let's focus back on the significance of Jerusalem…. Did you know that one of the greatest signs and wonders ever recorded in the Bible had to do with Jerusalem before it even came into the hands of the Israelite people as their possession? The story took place during the days of Joshua (Joshua 10:1-15.). In the Biblical account, the Canaanite King of Jerusalem headed up a ten nation confederacy to resist the forces of Israel who were being led by Joshua to conquer the land of Canaan. You see, at that time, Jerusalem was just a city in the middle of the land of Canaan, but it may have been the most significant one nonetheless, because the King of Jerusalem (during that time) was the one who was able to rally the support of the other nine Kings in the area. That says a lot! Anyway, a battle ensued, and the Lord helped the Israelites fight against the Allied forces of Canaan by sending down huge hailstones. The Lord killed more of Israel's enemies with hailstones than the Israelites did with the sword! But even more amazing was the answer to a prayer uttered by Joshua. He wanted more time to fight the battle that day, so he prayed for the sun and moon to stand still in the sky. . . And it happened! That unique day lasted nearly twenty four hours longer than usual[61] Never before or since (according to the Book of Joshua) had the Lord answered the prayer of a man, as he did that day for Joshua! That battle was the most decisive of all (in terms of the early history of Israel's mission from the Lord to 'drive out' the former inhabitants 'Canaan Land'. And it is interesting to point out again, that the allied forces against the Israelites were being led by the 'Pre-Israelite' King of Jerusalem.

I think I know why the Lord fought for Israel in such a spectacular way that day... The reason?.. It was all about 'Jerusalem'! Before the Israelites entered the land of Canaan to conquer it, the Lord told Moses (and the people) that a day would eventually come in their future when he would choose a specific place (within the borders of the Promised Land) to put his name ("pitch his tent", "hang his hat", and "settle down" so to speak). The plan was that in that "chosen place" the Lord would set up his platform of worldwide notoriety and fame, in order to draw all mankind towards himself that they might know him and be saved by him. Well, Jerusalem became that *"chosen place!"* You see, it was the *'King of Jerusalem'* who picked the fight against Joshua and Israel that day..., but it was *the Lord* who helped his people defeat the entire coalition in a matter of hours! I would imagine that the Lord may have already known at that time, that Jerusalem would become his *'chosen place'*. . .

And who hasn't heard of his fame? Who hasn't heard of "Jerusalem," and the "God of Israel" and all of his miracles?

CUT 6
The Six-Day-Wonders
A Sign At The End
Of The
Sixth Millennium!

. . . IN THE 'SIXTH' MONTH,
FOLLOWING 'SIX' YEARS AND 'SIX' DECADES
FROM THE START OF THE 20th CENTURY. . .
A WAR BROKE OUT IN THE MIDDLE EAST. . .
. . .THE WAR LASTED 'SIX' DAYS!

By the end of the conflict the Jewish people
had re-gained control over the ancient City of
Jerusalem and Temple Mount site (to whom it
had been lost for more than 2500 years![57]).
These were the events of the 1967 'Six-Day-War'
in the Middle East.

Oh yes, and one more thing. . . According to
the biblical timeline, the Six-Day-War took place
right at the end of. . .

'SIX THOUSAND' YEARS OF WORLD HISTORY. . .

WHAT'S UP WITH ALL THE "SIX'S"?

Fighting began on Monday June 5th when the Israelis launched a pre-emptive attack against Egyptian airfields, because of encroaching Egyptian forces. By noonday, air attacks by Jordan, Iraq, and Syria began. The Israelis began retaliating against the Jordanian and Syrian air fields. By June 6th the war was 'blazing', and by Saturday evening June 10th a ceasefire was agreed to by all sides, and it was signed on June 11th. It may be interesting to note that (taking account of *"leap years"*) the fighting which broke out on June 5th was actually happening on the *'sixth'* day of that month. This is because (in the leap year cycle) one quarter of a day is lost every year for three consecutive years every time a new leap year cycle begins. 1967 was the third year in the cycle, which means there would be 18 to 20 hours lag time which would push the 5th day of June 1967 into the sixth day (if the days were evenly spaced according to the actual time frame of a 365.25 day year. For whatever its worth, I'll let you *'rack your brain'* trying to figure out that one if you like! My point here is that it is all about the six's. . . i.e. A 'Six-Day-War,' June *'Sixth,'* the *'Sixth Millennium'* etc.! And if that isn't enough to chew on. . . Let me give you something else to think about in regards to the principal discussed in Chapter four *("The Heartbeat Of Creation")* having to do with the pattern of *"Six"* and the *"Seventh."* I believe that the "Six-Day-War" was a sign indicating that we are at the end of the Sixth Millennium and going into the seventh. The siege and capture of the City of Jerusalem and the Temple site by the Israeli army took place between the sixth and seventh days of June during the year of '67' ('6' and '7')!

CUT 7
D-Day
and the
Six-Day-War
'23 years"

By the evening of June 6th the Israeli army had totally surrounded Jerusalem with a siege, and asked headquarters for permission to take it at that time. The answer was no, but circumstances the next morning (June seventh) changed that decision. In essence the Israeli's *re-gained* control over the ancient City of Jerusalem on the *sixth* of June (by-the-way, this would add one more *sixth* to *"The Six Day-Wonders"* soliloquy).

But regardless of whether we add another "6" to the Six-Day-War, twenty three years earlier, to the day (June 6th 1943) marked the anniversary of *'D-Day'* in World War II. D-Day was the largest seaborne invasion in history, and it was a crucial turning point in the War. D-Day saw the landing of the Allied Troops on the beaches of Normandy France, which led to the downfall of the Nazis.

Both WW I and WW II resulted in the advancement of the aspirations of the Zionists. World War I ploughed up the ground of the Middle East, and World War II (and the Holocaust) resulted in the *planting* of the Nation of Israel in that Land.

But here is something *really cool.* . .   The timeframe between June 6th 1944, to June 6th 1967 is exactly 23 years. Those twenty three years made up the last *"one percent"* of the 2300 year spectrum, of the *Three-Way-Connection* from Alexander to the Six-Day-War!

CUT 8
The Sixth Millennium

I can't prove it, and it was not intended to be the main idea of this book, but I believe that the Six-Day-War may well have marked the *'official end'* of *'exactly'* six thousand years of world history (if we are calculating from the original *'360 day'* cycle of years.) Something to think about.

CUT 9

'One Third'

of the

"Stars"

Exploding Flywheels
A Millennial Fracture?

Some years back, research scientists were doing some experimentation with flywheels. They wanted to find out how much kinetic energy could be stored in a flywheel. When a flywheel spins, it stores energy, when it spins faster, it stores up more energy. In the experiments, the flywheels would begin to spin faster and faster, until they reached their maximum *'holding capacity'*. The experiments had to be done at a bomb testing site, because, as the flywheels reached the critical point, they simply fractured, and blew up!

Boom! The interesting thing is that when the flywheels fractured and blew apart, they did so in precisely three equal parts!

Perhaps the *'Millennial cycle'* suffered a similar type of fracture, or explosion, because of the angelic war, and the 2,333.333 year period of western civilization was the result! Just a thought. . .

CUT 10
Growing Up

Out or Up?
Which Way R U Growing?

t seems to me, that in business or profession, there are two different paths in which we grow. There is an *Up-ward* growth and *Outward* growth. You may have heard the old adage; *Find something you're good at, and do it!* In other words, find a level of proficiency, then grow and multiply on that level, and success will follow.

For instance, if you're good at washing windows, then wash windows. Step two: Start finding more windows to wash. Advertise on that level, beat out the competition, hire help, get more trucks etc. . . And as you grow and *multiply outward* on that level, your standard of living and personal wealth should follow suit. Soon, you'll be the best window washer in the community! And when people think of windows, they'll think of you! You may even become; *The King of the Window Washer's*!

Now I'm not trying to *make fun* of window washing, it's the same as the carpet cleaning profession (a profession, by-the-way, that I worked in, and really enjoyed). In fact, some years back, I met a guy in my church who about fifteen or twenty years later, who has been in that business for probably that same number of years, and he has made a *very good* living and was able to support his family well in that field of work. We started talking one day about steam cleaners and other tools of the trade, etc. It brought me back in the *Good Ole Days*!

Now, . . . People envy my artistic freedom, and creative independence, and I love the path I've followed. . . But *this guy* was in a *much more* comfortable position financially than I was. And as the conversation brought back *fond old memories*, I began to envy him. . . I was thinking to myself. . . *"I could've done that!"*

The Condensed Overview List
Seven Crucial Discoveries

1. (Page 60-62)

BACKGROUND: A Vision from the Prophet Daniel, which began with a scene of Alexander the Great and his conquest of the Persian Empire, predicted a *'restoration'* of the Sanctuary of the Jewish Temple in Jerusalem, after a period of time connected to the number 2300.

DISCOVERY: In 1967 (during the events of the Six-Day-War) the Ancient site of the Temple Sanctuary was restored to the Jewish people, exactly 2300 years from the time Alexander began his conquest of the Persian Empire.

2. (Pages 48-56, 64-65, 113-114, 231,and 246)

BACKGROUND: Ancient Christians (as well as many more Christians throughout Church history) believed that the flow of history is following a *seven thousand year cycle* (seven millennial days), and that Jesus will return to this world around the *end* of the *Sixth Millennium*, and rule the world throughout the entire *Seventh*

Millennium (after which time, a *new heavens* and *new earth* will be made.) This ancient Christian Worldview is called; *'Millennialism.'* Therefore, *'7000 years'* has been a very significant span of time, in the minds of many Christian believers.

DISCOVERY: The 2300 years from Alexander to the Six-Day-War, is precisely $1/70^{th}$ part short of being exactly $1/3^{rd}$ of seven thousand years. . . That's really close!

3. (Page 116-120)

BACKGROUND: A special '360 day year' is mentioned in the Bible (in contrast to the *actual* 365.25 day *'calendar'* year).

DISCOVERY: If we insert the *special* 360 day cycle of years, within the 2300 year period (from Alexander to the Six-Day-War), the 2300 years becomes exactly $1/3^{rd}$ of 7000 years (or, 2333.333 years), within the same year!

4. (Page 129-145)

BACKGROUND: If we add $1/70^{th}$ part (33.333 years) to the 2300 year period, from 1967 (in order to make a period of time equaling 'one third' of 7000 actual calendar years), it extends out to the year two thousand. From the year Alexander began to conquer the Persians, until the year 2000, seven empires have ruled the western world (in consecutive order).

DISCOVERY: If we divide the *new* 2333.333 year period of time into seven equal parts, it reveals   pattern. . . Like clockwork, the consecutive 'rise' and 'fall' of each empire repeats every 333.333 years.

5. (Page 222-227)

BACKGROUND and DISCOVERY: If we divide the 2333.333 year period into three equal parts, it reveals a pattern regarding the *'Three Great Eras* of Western Civilization': The *Classical Greco-Roman Era* (which *ended* with the fall of the City of Rome). The *Middle Ages began at that point, and continued until the renaissance*, and the *Modern Era* (which started with the Renaissance). The three divisions fall precisely on the *starting* and *ending* points of the *'Three great Eras* of Western Civilization.'

6. (Page and 228-230)

BACKGROUND and DISCOVERY: If we divide the 2333.333 year period in two equal parts, the halfway point marks the beginning of the Holy Roman Empire.

7. (Pages 220-225, and 246)

BACKGROUND: There are only two places in the Bible which mention an *'Angelic War'* involving Michael the Archangel. And there are only two places in the Bible which mentions *'stars'* that were *cast down to the ground* by an evil emissary. Both incidences are in the book of Daniel (in reference to the vision of 2300. . .) and in the book of Revelation (in reference to a *'War'* in Heaven). In the reference from the book of Revelation, the Devil swept away $1/3^{rd}$ of the stars of Heaven, and cast them down to the earth. I make a connection between the *"$1/3^{rd}$ of the stars"* in the book of Revelation, and *"the 2300 evenings and mornings"* in the book of Daniel.

DISCOVERY: In Millennialism, the lifespan of the *'Stars'* are 7000 years. So if *'all'* of the Stars of Heaven, were taken to mean *'all'* of the time of their existence, then '$1/3^{rd}$' of the Stars of Heaven would be 2333.333 years. Or put another way; $1/3^{rd}$ of the 'Stars of Heaven' represent 'one third' of the 7000 year Millennial Cycle!

Mike Darby lives in Angels Camp, California with his wife and two sons. Mike runs a gold panning adventure tour business in Angels Camp called; Gold Rush Originals, which is also his art studio. His wife Linda creates crystal jewelry.

(visit: goldrushoriginals.com)